Combat Survival Manual

Combat Survival manual, Volume 1

Mike Harland

Published by Mike Harland, 2024.

COMBAT SURVIVAL MANUAL

First edition. February 10, 2024.

Copyright © 2024 Mike Harland.

ISBN: 979-8224545636

Written by Mike Harland.

Combat Survival Manual

Book 1

Combat survival
Survival, Escape and Evasion, Tracking and Anti-Tracking

About The Author

I started training Karate in 1979 and continued for about 15-17 years, reaching black belt 2nd Dan in 1991. During this period, I participated in several karate competitions, winning gold, and several bronze medals in competition. From 1985-1986 we did my national service in the South African Defense Force (SADF), doing border duty for 9 months in the combat area (red zone/war zone). This is whereas a 20-year-old I saw my first contact (real life shooting) as a group of ANC/ SWAPO terrorists attacked our perimeter base.

From about 1987 till the early 90's I worked doing door duty at clubs, sometimes on my own and sometimes in a team. During this period in our country, you very seldom found men suing each other or presenting the case to the police, as they normally took their punishment like a man, and that was where I had most of my street experience situations up until about 40 years of age. Personally, and in the capacity of a soldier, Close Protection Specialist. I have used pistols extensively.

People mostly want to know what you based your training on and what experience you have. It is good for someone to ask because your life depends on the training you will receive from an instructor, you need to know that the person who is teaching you has experience in real combat. What does the person teaching you have to draw from as an instructor if he has no experience? Without a penchant for training in combat you will not have the will to succeed, you need a certain disposition.

1992 Started doing Close Protection (CP), which was a very new occupation in the public sector in South Africa (SA) at the time. There was not much in the way of sophisticated training courses for civilians. Whenever there was a possibility to train with an instructor that knew what he was talking about in CP, we would jump at the opportunity. During the period 1992 till 2005 I attended 4 separate CP courses and several other related courses such as shooting in low light, advanced foot and vehicle drills, Improvised Explosive Devices (IED) recognition, unarmed combat, knife fighting, and numerous others. These instructors ranged from civilian instructors to ex Special Forces (SF) and FBI certified instructors that were in the private sector at the time. During my CP experience, I have looked after celebrities, businesspeople, royalty, and diplomats.

During the years I worked as a close protection specialist, I had the opportunity to apply skills learnt to prevent IEDs being placed in areas around a venue. I was able to apply IED recognition experience in counter terrorism operations. In 2000 I was tasked to produce a plan to minimize IEDs being placed in The V & A Waterfront in Cape Town.

South Africa has a tradition of hunters and shooters because of the nature of the land and its tumultuous history over the last 300 years, where hunting and fighting were the order of the day, and this gave most South Africans a good taste of reality in combat. Therefore, it was more likely that we would be exposed to weapons living in South Africa, like the USA, we still have the God given right to defend ourselves *as should all first world countries' citizens.*

From about the age of 9 I had already shot with numerous weapons – basic lessons learned at such a young age are normally kept for life. My understanding was further developed by training in the army and being exposed to fully automatic rifles and heavy weapons, such as the 12.7 mm Browning, and this gives one the understanding of capabilities of the smaller and larger calibers of military weapon systems.

High threat CP is commonly referred to as Private Security Detail (PSD), and during 2004 the conflict in Iraq attracted a lot of PSD operators from all over the world. During my time in Iraq, I was able to use my issued rifle in close situations having to deal with the threat that sometimes materialized during our daily operations.

You soon learn it takes a ***determined, focused, and deliberate mindset balanced*** with self confidence that will allow you to win in a real gun fight; there is no room for negative thoughts or thoughts that detract from the winning, orientated, and focused mind.

When you train for combat it helps to train instinctively and to train so you react and do not have to think about tactics, because there is only time for reacting. With training you can speed up your mental calculating process; you can do this with intensity training that allows your brain to run through hundreds of options in a split second to conclude that best suits your dilemma.

My experience with martial and unarmed combat spans about 40 years where I trained not just with Karate systems but also to a minor degree Aikido (which is not a self-defense system), Judo and some ground fighting. My weapons training was with various weapon systems, handguns, and rifles etc. which spans about 29 years. To better understand where my skill level was in terms of international standards, I did an advanced certificate in handgun and rifle skills to round off my weapons qualification. This certifies a person to teach to an advanced level anywhere in the world and is internationally recognized

My Close Protection experience covers 17 years during which I did most functions of a Close Protection operative. This manual is based partly on experience, research and learning from others. I am not a survival expert but have hunted and have military experience and many years' experiences in teaching weapons unarmed combat and I have taught antipoaching as well.

How to use this manual

This manual is for survival and surviving a volatile situation (known widely by in the tactical and security industry as a "shit hits the fan" (SHTF) situation).

This manual is structured in a logical sequence based on the numerous considerations for preparing for and succeeding in various survival contexts. We begin with preparation of the individual, namely physical and mental preparation, as well as covering the equipment options available. We'll look at critical equipment as well as auxiliary options.

The manual also covers combative topics relating to survival in scenarios where hostile people may impact your operations and overall outcome. I have published other manuals that go into much more detail on topics of weapons, weapon training, combative capability and tactics, security and surveillance, vehicle operations, etc.

For those who read and enjoy this manual, contact me and get any of my manuals on Amazon or Draft to Digital online for a 25% discount. The manual will be supplied in PDF format.

*Keep in mind this is a basic manual, and advanced techniques and tactics are taught only on a course where we can see who is getting the information as we **do not teach criminals** or insurgencies that disregard innocent people. This **includes governments** that disregard the rights of their citizens. The only subject covered in detail herein is the Escape and Evasion (E&E) section, even though some advanced aspects are left out of that too.*

All writing in RED is essential or very important so keep this in mind as you read the book, this accentuates the most important aspects.

Read the whole manual and then decide what aspects you want to use for your specific environment and situation. You might need more of the survival information, and some readers might want to know more of the combat stuff.

When you see things repeated then it is very important and is repeated **<u>for your benefit</u>**.

With all practical subjects it is good to ***get out there and apply these techniques*** and learn the nuances of applying them. You will learn the aspects or functions and robustness of your equipment that you can only learn from using them. If you do not get out and learn what you can do and cannot do, it might be too late when you have a real situation.

This might seem obvious, but many people feel because they have equipment, they can use it correctly. It just does not work like that in real life. You must train and experiment to get the skills needed to survive.

This I see a lot, e.g., when teaching weapons training, I have noticed **people carrying a handgun assume they can defend themselves with very little training or even none.** Then in a real situation or test they perform hopelessly inadequately and either end up dying or barely surviving or failing the test. Using your equipment in training will demonstrate its weaknesses and shortcomings and how to use it most efficiently. This is if your training is balanced with technique, tactics, and stress management with regards to high stress situations like an attack by a mugger or in a SHTF situation. What I have also noticed is that ***if your technique is very good*** and you understand what makes for good accurate ***shooting or fighting*** then it normally ***stays with you for a very long time***. Granted it does take about a year or two to drill the techniques properly.

One very important survival aspect is to know how to **efficiently make a fire**, this seems simple but can be difficult if your hands are frozen from the cold, the wind is blowing, and your mind isn't functioning properly due to fatigue.

Do not try to learn too many skills at once, learn a few then practice them. This will help you to focus on the technique, as when trying to learn multiple skills you end up doing half a job and when you need them you cannot apply them properly.

Simple things to learn that would normally be easy in a calm and relaxed atmosphere can be extremely difficult to perform in a life and death situation, because the **stress can compound the problem** and cause you to make mistakes. For example, a pistol draw is easy when there is no pressure, versus trying to do it in an adrenaline pumping situation. This is due to your propensity to rush when in a life and death situation. Tension is another factor that diminishes your abilities in a combat situation, this is muscle tension which is induced by the stress/tension caused by the situation.

It is therefore imperative to have a good ***knowledge and ability*** (capacity/skill) before going into a survival situation. This can be achieved with a couple of months committed to learning basic skills to find water, make fire and make shelters. **An excellent skill to develop is the ability to <u>calm down</u> and think logically, patience is important, take your time and develop a good plan of action.**

Set aside 2-6 hours every weekend to test and learn these techniques.

That is the only way to give yourself the maximum chance of survival. If you have very little time in your days and no off time, then get some instruction on the very basic and most important aspects of survival and hope you make it one day in a survival situation.

Take one aspect at a time of this learning manual to train it into your mind. For instance, when making fire, you can first learn to make a good fire having all the right ingredients. E.g., cotton balls with Vaseline, then grass, very fine twigs, larger twigs the size of your finger and large logs the size of your arm.

- Making fire with a lighter is at times not as easy as it might

seem, try this first
- The next session you can work on making fire with magnifying lens
- The next lesson you can make fire with a fire steel
- Once you have those down then try friction fire

As I am based in Africa, this manual has many examples of an African nature, but you can easily adapt the concepts to other continents.

Here is an excerpt (passage) from a US training manual – notice the emphasis on experience:

What is the quality and background of the instructors? At a minimum, instructors must be highly skilled and be able to demonstrate mastery of the subject matter they are teaching. **Ideally, instructors should also possess extensive personal experience in real-world combat scenarios.** Not only will a skilled instructor do a better job of planning and conducting training, but elevated levels of experience and professionalism also motivates students to take training seriously and give maximum effort.

How many actual repetitions or iterations does each trainee perform? Whatever the training task might be, from assembling a machinegun, calling for indirect fire or leading a patrol, how many times does each trainee get to run through the process? Running through once or twice is almost useless. **For some physical activities even one hundred iterations are useless.** If training does not focus on letting trainees actually **do the task over and over it is not good training.**

End of excerpt

Fitness Considerations for Survival

12

Objectives

This section describes a basic calisthenics and cardiovascular program for survival. This program will also give you well-balanced all-round fitness.

The idea is to improve the student's overall fitness by applying sound principles that allow the whole body to be conditioned. To improve the body's ability to perform speed movements. To improve fluid movement, and this depends a lot on flexibility, it is important for the student to **apply stretching to their own personal training as consistently** as possible which should be if possible 15 to 20 minutes every day or at minimum 10 minutes 2-3 times per week.

This is not a comprehensive program, only a guideline to training for basic fitness to perform in a combat situation or general survival situation. For specific fitness such as pertaining to specific sports, your program will differ in that it will have coordination drills and specific technique drills for whatever sport you are training for.

Benefits of Fitness and Conditioning

This section is to clarify how fitness and physical preparedness will benefit you and help to get you through a survival situation.

1. Cardiovascular fitness will give you more endurance in a prolonged combat situation; this will become apparent in a sparring session when practicing combative drills.
2. Strength will give your body resilience to strikes and impact. The best way to get stronger without getting too big is to do light weight exercises with high repetitions.
3. Flexibility will help recovery from training, minimize injury and help with fluid movement in your body tissues. It also influences your speed by allowing the muscles to relax and contract more forcefully. Flexibility also allows you to do a full movement when executing a technique.
4. Balance improves by doing balance related exercises. This exercise also helps develop your core muscles. Balance helps to keep you on your feet in a combat situation and is important for high kicks, throws or takedowns, most striking techniques, and walking on rough terrain.
5. Power exercises help with power output with regards to fighting, or e.g., just running quickly after prey when hunting when you might have just shot at the animal and maybe wounded it.

Specific Exercises for Combat (Basic Format)

1. **Body weight exercises** will develop maximum power without developing any part of your body out of proportion.
2. **Light high repetition weights** will improve strength and help with muscle endurance when striking or using an axe, carrying a backpack etc.
3. Power exercises will help strengthen your core and give you the ability to use your large internal muscles for striking. Do power exercises on Monday and Friday to give your body a rest in between. Do light high rep or specific strength on other days e.g., cardio such as swim /run.
4. Sprints are a more **specialized exercise** and appropriate if you are going to a combat environment
   a. *Specific to combat survival*:
      i. 50-meter sprint (this has a specific purpose)
      ii. 100 or 200 meters
      iii. 400 meters sprints (for combat this will **take you out of effective range** of the average infantry man). This applies to survival in a war zone not in a basic survival situation.
5. **Dead lifts are** for raw power to lift heavy weights like a heavy backpack, tree, etc.
6. Squats: strong legs are needed for walking with a backpack, especially long distances, or for carrying someone in an emergency.
7. Dumbbell weights: swung at various levels and arcs

stimulate *core muscles* and connective **muscles, sinews, and tendons** for punching, carrying weights such as weapons, heavier tools like an axe, etc.

8. Plyometrics: develop power and the ability to perform fast movements.

Core Muscle Development

Basic bodyweight exercises should be done every day or at least Monday to Friday; this means 4 to 6 days per week is a guideline. Basic bodyweight calisthenics exercise, if done at a very intense level, can be done over 3-4 days a week for a sustainable program with good performance improvements. Cardio can be done depending on time available and fitness level for 3 to 6 days per week. This builds lung and heart strength and is very important in any SHTF type scenario.

The repetitions of body weight exercises (calisthenics) depend on your level of fitness. Basic body weight exercise is mentioned below. The ones listed here are the core body weight exercises as there are more exercises than these that you can do. Basic level would be 10 to 15 reps per exercise and an intermediate level would be from 20 to 30 reps (roughly) and anything from 40 to 80 repetitions is advanced (professional athlete/serious survivor). Except for "chins" where 10 is good and 15 to 20 is very good. When you first start doing chins only do 1 or 2 full chins at a time, then rest or do another exercise. Do this till you have done about 10 repetitions in total

The following movements can be done with explosiveness to get a plyometric effect.

1. Pushups wide, this can be done with a push off the floor with explosive movement for plyometric effect
    a. advanced push can be done in handstand positioning
2. Pushups narrow
    a. advanced push can be done in handstand positioning

1. Dips
2. Sit-ups (do quickly)

1. Chins (a.k.a. "pull up") narrow body vertical

1. Chins body parallel to ground
2. Squats
     a. Wide
     b. Narrow

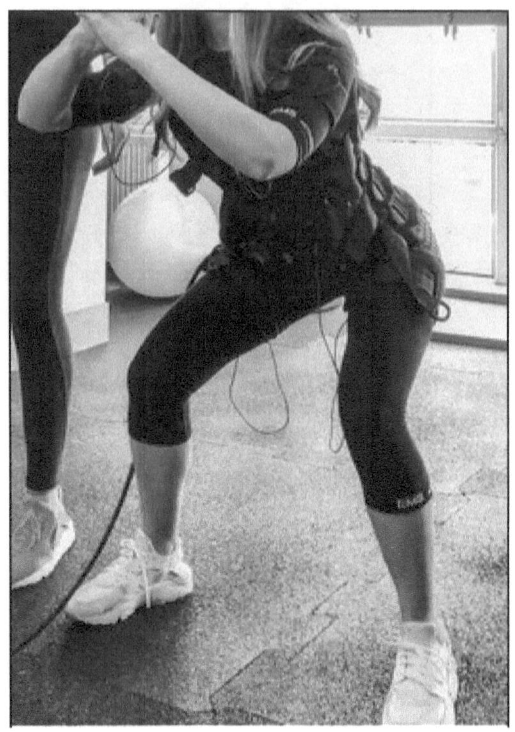

1. Lunges are good for the glutes, for sprinting and general fitness

Picture of an advanced lunge (a.k.a. Bulgarian split squat):

All movement exercises should be applied every day for at least 15 to 30 minutes depending on your level of fitness. Once your basic strength and fitness is developed after 6 months or 1 year then you can start with plyometrics.

Example jumping off a box and onto another or just off the box with a small jump after landing:

Repetitions

For ***muscle endurance the exercise would*** normally involve a weight such as a dumbbell weight, and 'basic level' repetitions will be 15 to 20, 'intermediate' will be 20 to 40 and more than 40 will be 'advanced' level. This does, however, depend on the amount of weight you are using and your level of conditioning.

Repetitions for power exercises will normally only be 5 to 8 repetitions as it puts a strain on the body, because it is a maximal effort. This is very important to build tendon (muscle to bone) and ligament (connecting bone to bone), over a joint.

Guidelines For Exercising

1. Warm up before training hard, this can be a long walk of 1-2km or a very slow run 1-2 km or light skipping. In a gym, you can use a treadmill to cover this distance conveniently.
2. Stretch lightly before exercise with **ballistic stretches** such as leg swings back to front or side to side, at the beginning; and harder at the end of exercise.
3. Drink enough water before and after exercise to stay hydrated. But **do not overdo water** as your body does not need as much as has been suggested over last 60-70 years.
4. Breath out on the effort and breathe through the nose where possible. You can inhale through the nose and exhale through the mouth.
5. Try not to eat before training because when the training gets harder you will feel uncomfortable and will not be able to perform. The body will be busy with digestion instead of sending blood to the muscles.
6. Power exercises should be **done once or twice a week** and the rest of the time light high repetition.
7. All exercises should be *done with full movement*. This is so you work the whole muscle and not just the short-range muscle.

Eat fruit salads and vegetables to have minerals for muscle function and carbohydrates for energy. Protein to repair muscles can be eggs, fish, chicken, steak, as well as a protein drink. Prefer protein from whole foods that are grown naturally without hormones, sprays, toxins, and other toxic substances. **Make sure it is not GMO as these GMO plants are <u>toxic.</u>**

Monitoring Your Fitness

This measures your Cardio Fitness:

1. Taking your RHR (resting heart rate) indicates if you are improving. When it lowers you know your heart is getting stronger.
2. If there is a sudden increase in heart rate by 10 to 12 beats it could be over training or an infection such as a cold.
3. Take your HR at the same time each time e.g., morning or evening. Try to make sure the situation is the same. Do not take after running and then in the morning as this will make it vary greatly.
4. A resting heart rate of 60 beats per minute or less is good. This indicates your heart is working efficiently and is not under strain and compared to an unfit person because your heart is beating 100 000 beats per day less. The average is between 74 to 84 for unfit people.
5. A healthy person could have a blood pressure of 120-140 systolic over 65-80 diastolic ***depending on your genetic predisposition.*** Do not stress if your blood pressure varies slightly as this is perfectly normal. You do not need to give the pharmaceutical companies money for **a naturally acceptable phenomenon**.
6. Measuring HR (heart rate) to see its response toto stress of exercise and external stimulation such as an attack.

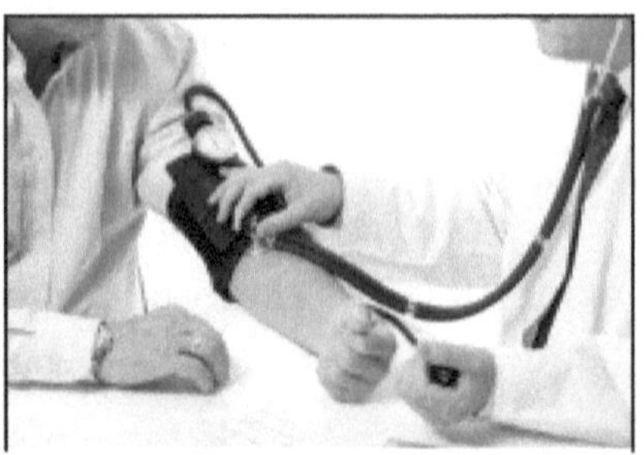

Increase in your ability to do repetitions will indicate your increased strength which is your ability to do more work. This is not so much about power but more about muscle endurance and strength.

Basic Program Design

1. **Warm up** without stretching is fine, walk about 1-2 km to get the body ready for the exercise, which can be on a treadmill.
2. Do repetition exercise for conditioning such as mentioned above.
3. For **advanced** students: core muscle exercises for 10 to 20 minutes.
4. Main exercises for unarmed combat: [choose one or two of the following exercises]:

a. Bag work (good cardio)
b. Shadow sparring (this is only good for distancing, timing, and strategic movement)
c. Repetition punches or kicks (these can be 30 to 50 reps)
d. Power punches (these can be 5 to 10 reps)
e. Sparring with a partner (duration will depend on students' fitness level)
f. Movement drills, this could be moving forward sideways out of line of fire of attacker's punches
g. Strategy exercises such as combinations or timing drills etc.
h. Breakouts for

i. Standup
ii. Groundwork

1. Hard stretch for 20 to 30 min (if times does not allow then 10 min will do). If you stretch each muscle once then you can stretch the muscle for about 1-3 minutes, this could be static (holding it) or ballistic (with movement).

Specific Training for Backpacking and or Combat Survival

Using and testing your backpack is essential to using it effectively in a real-life situation. The basics are just packing it with what you feel you will need for your area of operation/survival (desert / forest / jungle) and other survival equipment, such as water purifiers, shelter, insect repellent. Keep in mind *each person's terrain is different* and their *needs* and *experience* is <u>different</u> so the only equipment layout I can suggest is a **basic equipment list** as you will see in this manual, but each person must decide for themselves what is needed in their terrain, it might be a lot of water, or food maybe even ammunition as your situation might be a SHTF type scenario.

You will use the backpack, belt webbing and chest webbing for SHTF type situations. This will show you where *to adjust the straps* and how to adjust the webbing for the weight distribution and position of the pack and webbing.

Start with a light weight of 10-15kg for the beginning program (if you are at an average fitness level) and use this **till it becomes comfortable**, and your body gets used to it. This might take 1-3 months to get fit. Once you have this down you can start to push the weight up to 15-20 kg, you can continue to do this till you can carry about 10 kg heavier than you will carry on your outing/adventure. Try not to add more than 3-5 kg at a time. You will find that even 1-2 kg can make a big difference in how the pack feels and how tiring it is to carry it. The trapezius muscles take a lot of punishment when using a backpack and chest webbing. So, if you want to carry a 30kg pack in a SHTF situation then **train with 40kg**. This will give you an advantage over people that do not do this type of preparation.

You cannot just have handgun skills and a bit of fitness you need more than that. Camouflage, basic tracking and anti-tracking skills, rifle, and hunting skills. Survival skills such as making fire and basic shelter skills.

Keys To Survival

Important factors that determine success:

1. Any skills worth learning are **<u>worth learning properly.</u>**
2. There is no teacher <u>like **experience**</u>, so practice.
3. **Your mind** is the deadliest weapon in your whole arsenal of weapons and the most powerful survival tool and the **best tool for survival is knowledge.**
    a. Your mind is made stronger when you push yourself in exercise, by this I mean do as many techniques as possible, or learn a particular technique, like how to make shelter, and do it over again till you get it right and it becomes efficient.
    b. Learn by doing. This could be a climbing a mountain with backpack, swimming a river, carrying a very heavy pack after proper conditioning etc.
    c. As your strength increases, you will have increased confidence in your ability.

You feel more confident when you know more about survival, the terrain, have the correct gear and mindset which comes from confidence borne from understanding.

1. **Good health** such as general health and fitness determines whether you like to get out there and train.
2. **Mental focus** could be genetic or inculcated through environmental factors. You need to set aside time to get out there and train.
3. **Work through** things slowly, don't rush, initially it is about understanding then once you know then try to do it

faster.

4. **Try to understand** the technique as much as possible and
    as perfectly as possible.

Survival techniques are taught **to increase your survival ability**
when finding yourself stranded and in a dire situation, because of
a vehicle breakdown, air crash, shipwreck, earthquake, getting lost
while hunting or on a walking safari etc.

The most important aspect to remember is to **practice all skills
you have *been taught*.**

The techniques you apply in a realistic situation must make you
efficient at survival, not just capable. You can be capable of making
a friction fire. But it is not very efficient if it takes you 2 hours when
lighting a fire with a match or fire steel, as it takes only 2-3 minutes
to gather some fine grass and small sticks. Efficiency means you deal
with everything with a calculated and relaxed focused mind and
doing the technique without conscious thought. To achieve more by
doing this than running around in a panic, stay **calm** and **THINK.**
This is only possible if you train it.

The reason they use **acronyms** in survival guides is ***to focus your
mind*** on the things which are a **priority**. These make sure that your
priorities are more focused such as cover (shelter) for warmth and
fire to cook and sterilize water, as well as the sequence of the steps
you take to reach your goal.

Applying the ***basic rules*** will give you a guideline to follow, even
though **each situation will be unique** and should be treated as such.
For instance, it might be more appropriate ***in an African*** context
to ***get a weapon before looking for water***, food, or shelter. This is
directly proportional to the threats you will face as in Africa the
wildlife can kill you, the locals can kill you, certain snakes can kill
you, the landscape is harsh and can kill you, so arm yourself then
look for water, shelter (with fire) and then food. In the UK if you are

stuck out for the night and day you will not have to worry too much about the locals or animals, water is more abundant so shelter and food would be a priority.

Important note: *Make sure you are physically fit* and have practiced all your survival techniques before finding yourself in a survival situation.

Survival and Combat Skills Checklist

1. Tracking, knowing how to track enemies and wild game for food.
2. Weapons training
3. Unarmed combat
4. Communications, these should be overt, talking openly on a radio and encrypted comms
5. Anti-tracking, use of alternative footwear e.g., changing from boots to running shoes and for anti-tracking you can use wool sheep skin feet/boot covers. ***This will dull the outline of the foot*** /boot print and make the print appear old.
6. Navigation, such as using stars and sun to indicate direction then map and compass and lastly using GPS.
7. Plant recognition, this will allow you to survive indefinitely in the area you are operating in. Knowing your area of operation is imperative in many ways, food, cover and hides, avenues, and ways of escape.
8. Camouflage: knowing how to camouflage your hide (OP/ LP) your equipment and uniform, boots etc.

Supplementary Survival Skills

Besides the fundamentals, you might acquire some or all of the following skills to increase your chances of survival success.

Skinning Game and Tanning Leather

Skinning animals can be useful when hunting if the survivor is in a civil unrest situation that is ongoing. This is to make items of clothing in a long-term program. Jackets and outer clothes will protect your shirts in a long-term survival.

Extensive Knowledge of Plants

Here the knowledge of mushrooms and other edible plants will help in the long-term scenario where you will need to use as many of the resources available in your area. **Knowing the poisonous plants** in your area would be very useful as well as plants used for insect repellent.

Emergency Survival Medicine

Especially how to deal with cuts, muscle soreness, basic infections and controlling them such as flu, colds, foot fungus, and general hygiene. Treating hypothermia and heat stroke. Dealing with a drowning victim.

Learn Meat Preservation

1. Drying
    a. Biltong (a South African term; known as "(beef) jerky" in places like the US)
    b. Pemmican (this can last for years if prepared properly)
2. Smoking meat (red meat/pork) fish. Can give you an extra few months of food preservation
3. Salted (pickled in a wooden barrel or glass jar)

Water Proofing of Garments, Boots, Tents, Tarpaulin ("tarp")

An old style of waterproofing of garments can be very useful in a SHTF situation e.g.,

    a. bees wax 16 oz
    b. boiled linseed oil 8 oz
    c. turpentine 8 oz

Weapon Skills

For any type of civil unrest or SHTF scenario, weapons training is essential for hunting and fighting.

Reloading Modern Firearms and Black Powder Weapons

This is specialized and can be complicated if you do not understand what you are doing, it is also dangerous so before you start learning as much as possible and start slowly and build up as you learn more.

Black powder hunting is more for fun as modern firearms are very advanced and can hit game out to five hundred meters if you know what you are doing. But this is not what you are looking for as you want to hunt in a SHTF situation so a small caliber and large caliber rifle will supply all your needs.

Small Team Tactics

This is what you need to know when you work as a team, for patrolling, reconnaissance, hunting, and operations such as ambushes. Small team tactics are for operations where you need to find information on an enemy camp/venue or area. These allow the team to work seamlessly with each other with minimal communications.

See my pistol and rifle manual on Amazon or PSD manual online

Get 25% off my books if order PDF **directly from me**

Basic to elite pistol training: https://www.amazon.com/dp/B0851KJKZT

Advanced Bodyguarding: https://www.amazon.com/dp/B0B28KJ44K

Advanced Rifle manual: https://www.amazon.com/dp/B09K21LXR3

Camouflage manual: https://www.amazon.com/dp/B095GSFZTM

Trapping Game

This is a skill that will mostly be used when in a prolonged survival situation. This is not necessary when having to survive in an emergency as it would take only the basic traps to get game for food. The very important aspects that you must know is *where to put the trap*, how to set it up and how to not put your scent on the trap, the height of the trap.

Learning Survival Techniques

To realistically learn and be able to apply survival techniques means, you should not learn more than 2-3 techniques per day in 2-3 different disciplines (this is even pushing the limit, it depends on the complexity of what you are learning as well), so it can sometimes benefit you more to do 2 techniques for fire making and 2 ways of finding or getting water then this will help you to **remember** and **retain** the information so you can actually use it when you need to in an emergency. Keep in mind because it's a practical subject it takes a lot of time to apply lessons leant and to ingrain them so they can be used in an emergency. Like all techniques and tactics that are applied in a stress situation they must be second nature to be able to apply them.

This means that over a period of 2 days you should learn only about 3 - 4 techniques in total. Keep in mind if you don't learn the survival techniques correctly you might end up not being able to apply them in a survival situation. Learning different skills sets (survival, tracking, foraging, trapping) means you can learn more, but it is still limited by the amount of info you can learn in a short period of time. You can also only absorb a limited amount of information in 1 day. So, to apply techniques you need time, that's why you can only do a limited number of techniques.

This is also why focusing on the absolute essentials for survival first is essential then as you gain skills and ingrain them you can go onto more skills and technical aspects such as complicated traps. Keep in mind *it's a matter of efficiency that dictates you learn the basic survival skills first* and focus on these. Once you have all the basics under your belt you can focus on more advanced training. *This doesn't mean you can't learn more techniques* in each period, it's just less likely. Complicated skills such as figure 4 traps with complicated and sensitive trigger mechanism is for long term training, whereas minute details and basic facts can be learnt slowly, such as where to find water, making traps are more complicated and will take more time to learn. So only learn 4-5 types of simple traps such as a loop snare that can catch anything – these are simple and easy to apply and learn.

There are also limitations when instructing large groups because **each student needs a certain amount of personal instruction** to learn the basics. Some of the techniques could take a few hours just to understand and apply so for instance the fire making with the friction method depends on the types of wood in the area and the hardness thereof, as the base plate / board should be soft wood and the rotating stick slightly harder to create and ember. It takes time to get an ember, it can take an hour or so if you don't know how it works. It will also take some time to find the right woods for a friction fire and for this you might have to experiment to find the right woods as each area will have different trees.

Bushmen can get an ember up and have a fire going in anything from 3-10 minutes (or less), but the **average Bushman has done it a couple of thousand times**. Bushmen (Koi San) are indigenous to the Southern African region and are used to ranging great distances in their hundreds of thousands (possibly as much as 5 million total), but when the Bantu came down migrating from the Congo region in 1800s, they killed off the Koi San as they moved more and more southward. The Koi San went from millions to thousands; this is due to rival Zulu chiefs such as Shaka and his predecessors as well as heirs.

Another aspect that you should understand is when a person has time to think about a technique as taught. **The person will tend to understand it better when they have had <u>time to sleep on it</u>.** Therefore, people tend to fair better doing a technique the next day.

Important note: an important goal to work towards for your survival training is to increase your expertise so you can survive

<u>with less</u> and less equipment and rely more on your knowledge and in this way, you can carry lighter and be more self-sufficient.

Advice from Miyamoto Musashi (Japanese swordsman)

In his book of 5 rings, he discussed sword fighting and constantly discussed techniques which he mentions you should *train constantly*. He also mentions to use your *peripheral vision* in everyday life.

Strategy Advice from Musashi

1. Be honest with yourself and others
2. ***Prepare now*** and train hard
3. Learn <u>many different arts</u> that are concerned with your direction of expertise desired
4. Learn as much as you can about different professions
5. Don't despair over mistakes, change them
6. ***<u>Trust your intuition</u>***
7. Understand what you see and develop this ability
8. The ***small details*** make the ability to understand the whole better
9. Do not waste time.

Strength of Character

Quote from Karl Von Clausewitz on Character

"By the term STRENGTH OF CHARACTER, or simply CHARACTER, is denoted *tenacity of conviction*, let it be the result of our own or of others' views, and whether they are principles, opinions, momentary inspirations, or any kind of emanations of the understanding; but this kind of firmness certainly cannot manifest itself if the views themselves are subject to frequent change. *This frequent change need not be the consequence of external influences; it may proceed from the continuous activity of our own mind; in which case it indicates a characteristic unsteadiness of mind.* We should not say of a man who changes his views every moment, however much the motives of change may originate with himself, that he has character. *Only those men, therefore, can be said to have this quality whose conviction is very constant*, either because it is deeply rooted and clear in itself, little liable to alteration, or because, *as in the case of indolent (lethargic/idle) men*, there is a *want (lack of = famine) of mental activity,* and therefore a want of motives to change; or lastly, because an explicit act of the will, derived from an *imperative(authoritative/overbearing) maxim* of the understanding, refuses any change of opinion **up to a certain point**."

How does this help you; one way is it asserts that changing your mind continuously and not being convinced to *have a goal stick to it.*

Basic Rules for Survival

Keep in mind ***some things happen simultaneously*** so while you look for a place to ***shelter*** you might come across a ***hunting implement*** or fire starter **tinder**, such as pine needles and pine resin, a bird's nest (fire starter to take an ember), pine (for resin for glue, pine needle tea) that can be shaved to give fine flakes that can be lit easily. The hunting implement might be a ***spear*** or fishing spear which has a different point to normal spear (easiest to find and make), catapult (easy if you have basic materials), throwing stick (very easy to find and use), blow pipe (you will need bamboo or hollow reeds) or a bow (long term survival as it is more difficult to make and use) that will take some making but it is possible with a bit of effort. These are simple and easy to make in a survival situation and would be considered kinetic energy weapons for small games.

While looking for shelter and a hunting implement *you might come across some water*. So, as we can see, your **mind should be alert to things around** you and you should **take any opportunity** to access water, food, shelter and find a weapon to protect yourself or catch food.

Do not grab the first stick as your spear; look around for a **straight** pole at least 5 to 7 feet long, depending on the type of trees around in your area. Use a longer pole if you are tall and a shorter pole if you are short, but this is a guideline – do not make it too short so that it can stab you in the face if you fall. Your spear can now also double as a walking pole. The width must allow your pointing finger and thumb to touch or slightly smaller as a rough guideline. This will help you to hold and use the spear to the best of your ability. Spears have been used by the Massai to kill lions so don't underestimate this implement.

If you want a noose on the one end of your walking stick to catch small game or snakes, then make sure it does not get in the way when you walk. You can, if you are very creative, make a funnel on the spear to shoot a small arrow if you brought some **surgical rubber** as part of your survival kit (something like spear gun rubber used in fishing/spear fishing). It should preferably be hard wood but some of *these hard woods* can be *quite heavy*, so you need to balance weight with strength.

Teaching Note

When training basic principles **use them as part of a scenario** and get the students to go through each aspect of the mental process in their heads and explain to the student/ instructor what they are doing and how they will apply their survival strategy. It is **very important to understand what you are doing** and **why,** so that it stays in your head as <u>just theoretical</u> *knowledge doesn't normally stay in your head for long.*

Scenario for Mindset and Mental Planning

Scenario: you are stuck in your vehicle and need to get out of the situation as nobody knows where you are and so they will not be coming to look for you. These points can apply both to combat survival and normal survival. Plan your actions for the next day or two and ***then submit it for discussion with the instructors***. Be as comprehensive as possible and think through everything thoroughly, a good way to plan is to think a few steps ahead, that is decide what to do in response to various events. Think as many steps ahead as possible.

Survival Guidelines

The following sequence is used to orientate yourself in a survival situation or E&E (escape and evasion; normally applied to military operations and not being caught by enemy combatants, and you need to escape which could, be SHTF or military operation).

Using all your body's senses

a. Look for food [e.g., berries], tracks [man tracks (potential enemy), game tracks], water [row of green trees], shelter [cave/tree]. ***Foods would be edible trees*** or plants such as dandelion, thin leaf plantain (both edible and widely distributed) also sour figs (South African low ground plant – it seems there is a variant of this plant on the Australian coast which is edible) are both edible fruit and the juice of the leaf is astringent and used for ***mouth wash*** for oral thrush. Look for other medicinal plants that are indigenous to your terrain, e.g., Aloe ferox (used as a laxative), Acacia Karoo tree widely distributed in Africa (used as emollient and astringent for colds and conjunctivitis). Animal tracks converging on a point will normally lead to water especially if towards a green line in the far distance as this normally indicates trees and a river.

Sour figs:

a. Look at the terrain and how you can traverse (cross) the terrain, e.g., can you go down river without drowning, are the mountains too far and too high to go over? Is the terrain passable to a person on foot, would you take a natural path made by animals and what would be the dangers if you did this? Dangers in Africa would be if you follow a game path (springbok) herd you will then also meet the predators such as leopards and lions, hyena, cheetah etc.

b. *Using your eyes*, you see the game trail. This means food, but when you consider this, you might not have the means to obtain food from a large buck such as a gemsbok, or springbok even if you see one and can stalk it. This is one reason I say make a spear first as it is the quickest to bring down a large animal (assuming you don't have a firearm, or bow, of course). There are smaller game species in Africa such as steenbok that are more manageable to hunt and kill. Even tough warthogs are small but very aggressive and can be dangerous due to tusks that can cause serious injury.

c. ***Listening to your environment means you hear the*** birds/ animals and herds of game running, warthog digging. ***The sudden <u>absence of birds singing</u> could be the presence of <u>a</u> <u>predator</u>.*** This is also a warning signal when there is a cacophony of birds singing and then all of a sudden you hear ***baboons barking*** making lots of noise as this is sometimes a leopard or lion. Keep this in mind when walking or hunting as well as doing general reconnaissance.

   ○ **IN SHTF <u>Listen</u>**. This could be for water for hydration/ escape, enemy, friendly forces (you will ***know their gunfire*** as ***different weapons systems sound different***) animals etc., you might hear marching, ***talking, engines*** (tanks are very loud), music etc.

Aloe Ferox:

a. **<u>Smell</u>**, this is because the enemy/other hunters could have
    a fire going nearby, the diesel from motor vehicles can be
    smelt for one hundred or more meters depending on
    amount released into the air. Then the obvious smells you
    will have when nearing a village like the smell of farm
    animals, fires cooking and such. One of the reasons soldiers
    are not allowed to smoke is it can be smelt for hundreds of
    meters and seen for a 1 km at night. This is how English
    snipers used to find and shoot Germans in the 2nd World
    War.

Size up your personal situation

a. **Where is your gear?** (pack it if it not packed yet), never leave equipment lying around *once used put it back in* the backpack, this would be implements such as eating utensils or *survival knife* put it in the *sheath immediately* after use.
    - especially binoculars
    - range finders which are used in certain reconnaissance or sniping operations
    - multipurpose tool
    - ferro rod when making fire, this can be left behind very easily, its best to tie it to your body

b. Just after a combat situation or contact check for medical problems such as **cuts, bullet holes,** as you *might have been shot* and *not even know* about it, this is due to *adrenaline.*

c. *Check your <u>weapon state</u> if this is applicable*, is the magazine full? Change it if it is not, replace magazines in your webbing. Replace empty magazines with full ones if you have a stock of spare magazines that are intended for resupply.

d. *Check your hide site* (listening post/observation post; or LP/OP) if this is applicable, this would mean *walking around and seeing if it gives good cover* and egress (moving out) and ingress (entry) avenues to enter the site without being seen. How much camouflage you can apply will depend on the time before dark (unless you have a night vision device (NV)) and the closeness of the enemy combatants. If the enemy are close, get into a large bush but first *make sure you haven't left sign* if possible. Use hard ground, grass, stream etc. Then enter the hide LP/OP otherwise you will just lead them to your position.

e. **Check for resources around you**, maybe some **tinder** for a
    fire later, is there **water** or **natural shelter** in case you need
    to get out of the rain, *get away from dangerous animals*,
    in SHTF get away from potential attackers. Is the long
    straight pole to make a spear anywhere close to you? *You
    might need to make a pack* if you do not have one, or
    improvise a water bottle, *look around to see if there is
    anything in your/other vehicle (car, plane, boat)* you can
    use for water carrier, cordage, cover for shelter, fire making
    (battery) etc. You might not have to travel far to find these.

Find out where you are

Look at a map, check your GPS for coordinates. If you know your area you can also orientate yourself to surrounding mountain ranges or landmarks. That is if you are familiar with the basic terrain where you are. *Identify mountain ranges*, rivers, and hills around your area to *orientate yourself*. Once you know what your position is you can orientate your map and then proceed to your destination by choosing an appropriate route.

1. If you do not know where you are, how will you know where you are going or even decide what your destination will be. A basic idea could be the mountain range leads to the town so follow the range. It doesn't always have to be complicated.

2. If you can establish where you are then identifying a road can guide you, then walk to an area with the highest likelihood of having roads leading to towns.

3. *Go in the direction where you will find <u>water</u>,* because where there is water, there is normally food, both plants to eat and animals to hunt. Water is sometimes indicated by a green line in the distance (vegetation).

4. If it is a combat survival situation or a country where you are a foreigner then you might not be treated with courtesy, *then move at night* and **<u>dress</u> and act as much as possible like the <u>locals</u>** do (clothes head gear etc.). You might need to find clothes, borrow them from a clothesline and move through the area. This will give you an increased chance of survival

Plan your movements

Study the terrain. ***<u>Here is a basic idea</u>*** E.g., move to mountains at night, rest there, look for water (mountains are good place to look for water due to mist / rain and pools are found around and, on the mountains) then next morning continue to the sea etc.

1. Your route might be dictated by a water source, cover and concealment or food, shelter, or security concerns such as where the enemy are or are not.
2. This is made easier if you know the general terrain or ***have a map with terrain features on them.***
3. While you are considering your options think of your **plan B** as well and other options if your way is blocked by terrain or a swollen river or mountain, even combatants (SHTF) etc. you might need to go around such obstacles. You might consider holding up for a period if the area has plenty of game and other food to eat, build your strength by eating and drinking, then move on when you feel stronger. **<u>Stretching</u>** is a good way to release tight muscles. Massaging your feet can also relax your foot muscles and increase blood flow to the feet. Massage and stretching will increase ***your ability to recover***.
4. Look after your general condition by getting enough sleep, food and water.

Get some sleep

Learn to sleep when you can in a SHTF scenario because you do not know what you might be doing in the next few hours, you might be running, fighting, foraging. So, getting rest is important when you can.

Rules for Team Survival

The number one rule when doing survival in a group is **each person does a chore** that will assist the whole group. There must be **no arguing or complaints**. If you want to, choose a leader or leaders as this might help but each person must be mature and do their bit for the team. If you are going to choose a leader, **find out if they have any skills** in the wild first.

1. **Each person** must sit down and **take stock of <u>their own situation</u>** and **their condition** (mental, physical, and spiritual). This means what is your state of mind, what equipment you have on you, did you injure yourself during a crash, determine now that you want to make it and work with other people. Take stock of food, water and other equipment, knives, guns, bags, shelters, axes etc.

    a. This is important because one person might have a lighter and another a few matches and one might have a fire steel. You can build a picture of what your equipment is.

    b. One might have a shelter and another a knife or machete (Panga/kukri)

    c. Someone might have a GPS and or a compass

    d. You might only have one or two backpacks amongst the group, you will need this to carry your equipment

    e. One of you might know about indigenous plants and this person should be designated to find and test to see if its edible, teach the others so everyone knows, especially if you know of a poisonous plant.

    f. As you can see knowing your status with regards

to equipment, food, water etc. will be an important step before setting off on your planned route.

    g. Share your knowledge and don't assume others in the group know what you know.

2. **Work together,** the whole group or designated leader must agree to the plan. If no consensus is reached then either you can split up or pick a leader for each team and go your own way by allowing the person who seems to know the most about survival, navigation (getting to safety) and security to lead the way.

    a. Don't have one or two people doing all the work as everyone must do their bit.

    b. Allocate those that seem most suitable to a chore, a big strong man should collect wood and a weak woman can work at your base camp with food. Shelter making is best for the guys as they have the strength to lift heavy beams for a shelter if this is needed.

    c. Hunting should be done by the person with most experience with this and strength to hunt and kill an animal if needed.

    d. Security should be the responsibility of the most experienced and capable of assessing these threats and developing a plan of action to negate these threats.

3. **Don't argue, it wastes energy and time**, decide to go with someone leading or go your own way, wasting time is counterproductive and you will have less time to hunt or travel. It also distracts you from security challenges. You need to have an awareness of your surroundings. This is imperative to survival and keeping your sanity as the

situation is very dangerous.

    a. Discussion can be heated especially in a tense situation like survival. This isn't necessarily arguing, just coming to a consensus.

    b. **Keep focused on the task at hand** as heated discussion can be constructive if you don't lose focus, which is getting to safety and survival in your situation.

    c. As many opinions as possible, it's better to have as many views as possible and ideas. This will give you options and can lead to a better outcome, so listen to other opinions and calculate from there.

    d. This doesn't mean everyone should discuss all aspects all the time. For instance, if you are blessed enough to have 2 or 3 security experts amongst your number of survivors then let them discuss the security aspects of the survival situation. Let the rest go about and collect firewood, or wild fruit and other foods etc.

4. **Help each other, teach,** and **assist, then you will get out faster.** A team gets stuff done quicker; at stops decide who collects firewood and who gets and cleans water, who gets local edible vegetation and who sets up the shelter. Who sets traps if this is relevant and who sets navigation goals?

    a. *Helping each other must be a principle* set out and explained so that everyone understands this and applies it. *If someone doesn't work together then they must be excluded from the benefits* of the other work till they come to their senses.

    b. Keep in mind if you are in a survival situation then working together is both *efficient and correct*, which is beneficial for the whole group.

Nobody must stand around doing nothing unless they are on OP duty which is a security function and needs the full attention of the operator/survivor.

c.   Making fire can take quite a lot of effort collecting firewood, and if **friction fire** is used it can be **very difficult** and time consuming if the wood is not appropriate (dry enough) and you don't have experience in making a fire by friction. Build up about 5 times what you feel you should need.

d.   Making shelter is or can be strenuous if you need to make a large shelter for a couple of people. Making a basic shelter sheet cover and a basic fire for warmth can make a big difference. Keep it simple and **be efficient**.

e.   **Security is more important than most aspects of survival** in a certain context and should be seen as important especially in a **war zone** / **SHTF type scenario** or civil unrest. Only let the most aware and trained persons do this function.

5. **Check each other's equipment** before leaving camp and check each other's backpack/Bergen *zips are up* and nothing is falling out while traveling along the route. *Make this a habit every 20 -30 min* or at least every hour when you rest and reassess the situation.

a.   This benefits everyone, as losing a compass can send you off in the wrong direction.

b.   Losing a weapon or ammunition can result in your deaths if you hit a contact and run out of ammunition.

c.   Losing a water canister can result in dehydration and lack of focus and death if you fall down a mountain because of lack of strength, coordination, and focus

    d. Catching a problem soon can also save you time if you notice a piece of equipment fell out then it means you can fetch it and carry on your way without losing important items.

6. **Communicate** to each other about what you are doing and ***where you are going*** so people don't get lost and nobody knows where others are e.g., was it to collect wood or to hunt? This will be both good for the team as it will save time looking for a person and safety so you can help if in need, it therefore benefits you and the team. You can leave trail markers or give a trail indicator on a map and or take radios and keep in radio range. Don't swear (use expletives) when communicating it wastes time and takes longer and can confuse the situation.

    a. ***Encourage honesty as lying can cause confusion*** and lead to a major security problem. If for instance a team member is seen by an enemy or person when hiding and they don't mention this because of embarrassment and then enemy combatants engage you due to this discovery, you could lose the whole team.

    b. ***Communicate where you are going*** and what your function is going to be as well as what time you should be back. Don't wonder off on your own without any warning to others, in a SHTF situation you might also get shot.

    c. ***The team leader must know where the person went*** and what their function was, communicating this directly is best but even sending a message if nothing else is also acceptable.

d. In some circumstances of war, civil unrest you might want to use *sign language* or *clicks* (made with the tongue), this is because *spoken words travel* far and can be heard in bush more readily than clicks. This is if the whole team know these signals.

7. <u>**Each person carries their own weight**</u> both their pack and figuratively (does their chores). Carrying 10% of your body weight is comfortable, but this greatly depends **on your physical capability** and fitness level. Women can carry 10 % of their own weight and men can carry 20% of their own weight as a guideline. **Don't let sick or weak people carry heavy** as this will make your journey slower and this will mean you will get to your destination much slower.

a. Carry your own weight and equipment. This has a few benefits, with more people carrying equipment you can carry more, such as 2 saws. Like a military team, everyone pulls their weight

b. Help injured or sick people till they are ready to carry their own weight, this is beneficial as once they are up and running again then they are an asset once again. If you neglect them then you might lose them and be one down. Obviously, those that are seriously injured might have to be left on the spot and a team of fit healthy individuals can try to reach a nearby village or town. Staying in place waiting for a severely injured person can be dangerous. Each situation will be different so make your decision based on calculation. Things such as availability of food, water and shelter will dictate whether you stay or go.

   c. Carry only **what you need** *as fatigue will make you more susceptible to mistakes.* In a survival scenario you just cannot afford to make mistakes.

   d. **Carrying** only what you need is *dictated by what your operational goals* are, if you carry exceptionally light on an ambush patrol you might run out of ammunition. Running out of ammunition during an ambush is profoundly serious as the enemy might have a tracker team and then you have to counter this tracker team. As you can see this will not turn out well unless you are very fit and can run extremely far and very fast.

8. **Keep your kit packed,** only take out what you will need to use for that specific job. If it is a fire take the fire making stuff out and pack it away immediately once finished. This is so if you must move then you can do this without leaving stuff behind. You might need to escape from or get away from an animal, flooding, fire, or enemy etc. This is why we keep the kit packed.

   a. If you cut wood with a saw or axe then **sheath it** and pack on outside of pack, this includes spades, or any other thing used in everyday use.

   b. This is just as important for binoculars used when in an OP (observation hide).

   c. Camouflage netting or shelter construction if not being used then pack it away.

   d. **Make a checklist** and work through this before you leave your camp every time you leave.

9. **Important note: check the area before you leave so that** a person doesn't leave a headlamp or fire-making equipment behind. This includes rifles as they are

sometimes left leaning against a tree or water bottles left in the stream etc. *Be consistent and take your time*, move slowly, and stay alert. This will include *checking your equipment <u>every 10-20 minutes</u>* so as not to lose equipment. This is efficient if you are using the buddy system where two operators look out for each other watching each other's back.

10. <u>**While in training on courses**</u> compare **kit** and <u>**learn from others**</u> what is available in equipment technology trends e.g., lighter Bivy bag, stronger and lighter stove etc. Sometimes it will be learning *what not to buy* or what not to take with, as <u>***advertising***</u> *and <u>**hype**</u> might have caused the person to buy an item that is useless*. This is where **testing all equipment before use** should have ironed out any equipment that doesn't work or is easily damaged. *Learn from the Bushmen – they carry <u>extraordinarily little</u> and know a lot about their environment.*

11. <u>Compare and improve kit</u>
    a. *This is because improvements are continually brought to the market as time passes, especially items such as night vision, thermal vision, backpacks, bullet resistant vest.*
    b. *Stronger and lighter equipment makes you more efficient as you carry lighter and therefore can do more with what you have.*
    c. *Better quality monocular, better waterproofing is going to make you more efficient and capable at monitoring your surroundings as an example of equipment improvement. Clearer glass helps you to identify the enemy from further and make reconnaissance easier.*
    d. *Better stronger more reliable weapon system will*

make you more combat efficient, if this is added to reliability and good combat (technique and tactics) training you have a winning combination.

e.   *Each person has their own understanding and learning means each person has something to add to the overall abilities of all. This enriches everyone if the training is made available to all. This is how most SF units will operate by using everyone's expertise to the maximum and learning as they go. This is of course limited to the abilities and experience of that special force's unit instructor. This is why some units do not perform at the same level as others.*

Rules for Single Person Survival

1. **Don't travel alone if you can help it**, but of course you don't plan for accidents, so these rules apply to single person survival if you find yourself on your own.
2. Sit down and take stock of your:

a. **Situation**, what's happening around you, who is around this is more important in 3rd world country as the crime can be serious and violent, where are they, what is their general attitude to outsiders (that is if you are in a foreign area) what is your geographic location, what *__direction is safety__*, *what is the best way to get there*

b. **Equipment**: have you got all your equipment that you carry in your vehicle or on your person, have you got everything that was in your vehicle/plane/boat, or have you lost anything from your bag/vehicle and what did you bring with you?

c. Condition, **were you injured?** Apply first aid if you are injured as any injury can become infected and because you more strain. __Dehydration__ can sometimes __sneak up on you in a combat__ or stress situation so **make sure you are hydrated** if it's possible to access water. Other precautions might be as simple as making sure you don't get injured, such as knowing how to safely use an axe/blade or keeping aware of snakes and other dangers.

1. Because you are on your own you should be __very aware__ of **your surroundings** as your survival depends on *it both from a protection point of view* and *finding water*, shelter, and food. This includes looking for predators and other wildlife dangers e.g., a rhino with its calf, or a hippo near

water. Watch where we step as you don't want to be **bitten by a snake**, when on your own or with other people, especially if there is no medical help close by. This should not normally affect you as snakes move away from people if they can hear/feel you (not always as e.g., *Puffadders are lazy*).

2. You need to have a *focus point in the distance* – ensure you don't walk in circles which can be due to your stronger leg which pushes off stronger and can cause circular routes. Find a focal point when you determine direction. Look for a hill, tree, or any other prominent feature in the direction of travel. Once you know the direction then you can choose which direction will give you the best chance of survival.

3. **Plan** for all things *within your capacity,* to do so. By this I mean if you don't have a compass and you don't know how to determine south by the stars then you cannot plan an accurate direction.

4. **Use rest stops for water and food** along your path as is possible. This is to keep your condition in the event of a contact with the enemy in a SHTF situation or just to keep your condition in a normal survival scenario. Water stops, to drink from streams, dams, or rivers where possible save your own water supply – hydration is especially important to be able to function properly. Rushing can cause you to make a mistake like walk into a heard of elephant or walk into a pride of lions.

5. **Look for sheltering places,** this means finding a place to rest and maintain your body heat and sleep and eats as well as hide from enemy if it's a combat survival situation. Make sure it **is not isolated with no escape routes.** Choose a place about 2 hours before Sundown so you can make

improvement, check camouflage, recon your E&E routes and do a recce of surrounding environment

6. Find **secure** places such as natural *hides or places of security for temporary* stops, also look for places to travel with cover, by this I mean good route selection either visually or on your map. (tall trees/caves/thick thorn bushes) to go to if you are in the *African bush* as it is *the most dangerous bush in the world*. It's full of deadly threats and dangers. It's not like getting stuck in Europe or America. LOOK, LISTEN, SMELL.

This rule takes it for granted that you are applying the *awareness rule* because even though you want to plan it still takes your mind to look and search out places to **temporary shelter** and a place to make fire **as you travel through the landscape** as the fire might need to be *covert* as in a **Dakota fire** (see section on fire making) which means you need very dry and thin twigs as well as an *area to dig the small holes* having a *tree above to disperse the smoke* will help as well.

1. **Don't take chances** not even when in a team but definitely not in a single man survival scenario. This is where a lot of people get hurt and end up having to crawl for miles to get help. Unless of course you're a TV "survival" celebrity like Bear Grylls and have a whole medical emergency team on standby (he likes climbing cliffs *he doesn't need to,* and falling from a cliff you didn't need to climb it is just dumb in any type of survival scenario – it's made for TV audiences). *You won't see e.g., Ray Mears doing that dangerous stuff. In reality you won't take chances* like you see TV survival experts take.

2. It's safer to have a **high shelter** than one on the ground if

you are one person especially in the African bush. This means on a ledge or in a rock hollow up on a slope, in a tree. If it's inaccessible, then ***it's hard for <u>someone to approach</u>*** or a ***predator to stalk*** and attack you and therefore easier to defend yourself in this type of height advantage. ***Just keep in mind leopards like caves and trees. Snakes like caves,*** as well as all types of insects such as ticks (diseases), scorpions (poison) and bats which carry disease but if you smoke it out it might be ok for the night.

3. **Keep your kit packed (this is a golden rule of operating especially in a SHTF environment)** only take out what you will need to use for that specific job in your backpack. If it's a fire you want to make then only take the fire making stuff out and pack it away immediately so if you must move then you can do so, this might be to get away from an animal, flash flooding, fire, savages etc.

4. **<u>Check the area before you leave,</u>** you don't want to leave your headlamp or fire making equipment behind. Not doing this might mean you need to travel 20 -30 km back to your last place of rest to pick up a left fire steel or other item left due to negligence

5. **Don't just approach anybody you see along the way,** especially if you don't know them as you are alone out in the wild, you might stumble upon poachers, and they might think you are security forces and shoot at you. This type of scenario has happened to travelers especially in third world countries. It might also be that the people you meet are the criminal element or as in a civil war type situation they might be jumpy even if they do not think you are the enemy the tension might cause a situation to get out of control. ***Keep in mind people don't act normally in an abnormal situation.***

6. Don't carry a heavy backpack in SHTF, it makes you **too tired to fight** if the situation is one of security and you are the lone survivor. This is where *caches are good or necessary to maintain physical integrity for combat*. If it's purely survival then it doesn't matter, carry what you feel you can manage. Keep in mind you can either cache your supplies along a route. But when are operating an area of operations in a survival or SHTF then you can cache heavy items and extra food or similar extra items whatever they are?

Mindset For Survival

You will be **fully immersed** in a **confusing** situation where **stress** and confusion are going to be *debilitating*.

Being lost is a very dangerous situation and can be deadly and that is why there are lost hiker rescue organizations all over the world.

The first thing to allow a positive outcome is to **assess your situation**, this is done *visually and through awareness* and considering your *condition* and your *equipment* layout.

Where are you (location), where is civilization (direction), what equipment do you have?

It is quite simple *you can only rely on your own wits and the skill* you *have learnt over the years*. This is going to be tough if you have not learnt any skills. On the other hand, if you bothered to go on a short survival course then you might just have a chance. If you have done extensive survivable training your stay in the bush might be an easy situation.

Any negative attitudes will only slow you down or drag you down so keep yourself from any negative thoughts and focus on threats at hand instead. These threats might be thirst or hunger, not necessarily nasty people; it might be very cold, so your shelter will be a focus.

The body experiences <u>slight lethargy</u> and <u>weakness</u> due to lack of energy as you might only have minimal food and therefore less energy. This is normal but for those not used to it will be more affected due to a combination of accumulated stresses from external factors e.g., weather either very hot or cold, enemy combatants, internal stress from lack of energy. What happens is, your *body gives off <u>adrenaline</u>* which helps you build shelter, hunt and forage for food as well as walk out of the situation.

This should be expected as well as lack of sleep, which is another external stress. When you lack sleep, the body gives off **adrenaline**; this kicking into the body will **heighten your senses** and *keep you from sleeping*, this will all *accumulate to cause major fatigue*. This must not come as a surprise and must not cause fear or apprehension. After about 3 days you will be very fatigued but after *about 1 week due to stress and fatigue you will sleep like a dead man,* and **you will start to synchronize** with nature and adapt to your surroundings. This can only continue for about *3 weeks of minimal food* then your body will *start breaking down*, bear in mind this is *very different for individuals* as everyone has different **fitness** and genetic **differences**.

Cold will be a real threat so shelter for warmth will be *important* or even the difference between *life and death in some circumstances*. This is a very stressful situation – if it wasn't stressful then it would be easier to get out of the situation alive. It is the nature of the situation that is stressful. Once you adapt and start to get into a rhythm then things will normalize to an extent if you have the ability to adapt. Normally either youth or fitness will allow the best chance of survival. Combined with this, at least some training or even better extensive training.

Either way, your mind should **not entertain negative thoughts** as it will not help anyway, so you might as well think how you will find food or make a fire. Keep your mind on positive aspects of survival. *Have a focused mind* don't just wonder off, **have a plan** and stick to it even if it is basic e.g., to "travel south and look for water", you should know which direction is "south". Basic navigation can be done using the sun as the sun rises in the east and sets in the west and if you are in the southern hemisphere *aim your watch 12 o clock at the sun* and *bisect the point between 12 pointing at the sun* and *hour hand* and that's north, so south is 180 degrees in the opposite direction.

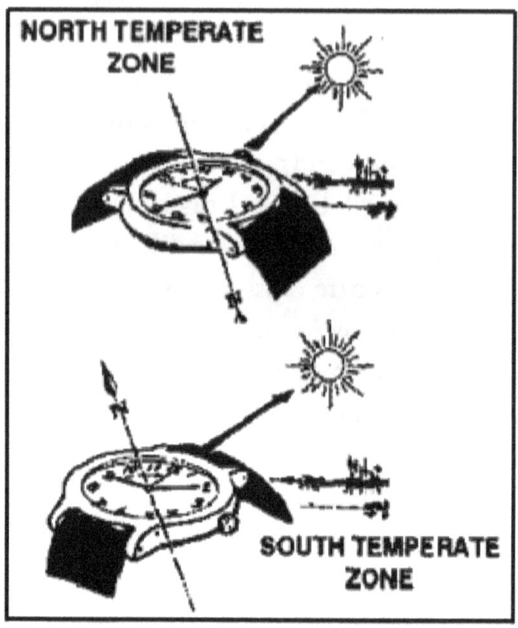

See below for another depiction of how to find "south" using watch

Survival Tip: Courage and Training

Quote from Von Clausewitz:

> "It is not our object to gain for these brave men a better lot–that would contribute nothing to their efficiency, and little to their happiness; we only wish to represent things as they are, and to expose the error of believing that a **mere <u>bravo</u> without <u>intellect</u>** can make himself distinguished in War."

This means that courage alone won't help you in SHTF or war but thinking and calculating combined with training will take you a long way to being successful.

Survival Priorities

82

Priority Overview

Personally, I believe the priorities **are <u>flexible </u>to an extent**; even though you will always need *shelter, fire, water, food*, and a weapon (a *weapon* is very important in *Africa*). The reason for these flexible priorities is that in an *African savannah scenario*.

It doesn't mean it has to be in any specific order as you might find water when you are looking for a shelter, as discussed above **<u>we are always aware of our surroundings </u>**so finding 2 or 3 of the priorities at the same time are possible but not necessarily probable. The priority means you need certain aspects of survival in place to maintain your body temperature, energy need, and hydration and therefore need have a fire, shelter, and water to achieve this. In what order you find these will depend on what you have in the terrain and what equipment you have on you.

Having a knife will allow you to build shelter and access food by building a small trap for small game such as birds, rabbits etc. If you can't find food in a jungle, then you really don't know much survival because it's got abundant life all around. These include scorpions, snakes, fish, birds, heart of palm, wild fruit and the list goes on. The next thing you would want to do is find a spear or make a bow, a bow can be used to fish as well as shoot birds or game. Even better for processing wood is a small folding saw

Another consideration for survival priority is how prepared you are before you get into the situation. If you were prepared then you have *3 ways to make fire, 3 ways to procure and clean water* with a shelter sheet for shelter, this means you can spend time on determining what route you take to get out of the situation and which direction you will take. You will have a few days' worth of food and maybe a few liters of water in a 3-day bag so this means your **<u>efficiency</u>** will go up and you are more likely to make it out without too much effort. Normally finding food and making a shelter could take you a few hours if you are not prepared. If you are prepared and know what you are doing and **have the necessary equipment** it could take you 5 minutes to set up a shelter.

Other things that will affect the survival priority is how far you are from help, if you are a few hours then no water or food is needed or 1- 2 days away from help then you won't need all the traps and food or fire, all it takes is walking out safely, so maybe needing a *spear* will give you the *defense capability* you need *while walking*. Then you travel to the place where the help might be. It would help if you knew navigation, such as where north is, so you don't wander off into the unknown aimlessly. So, we can see survival priority depends on the situation and preparedness as well as where you are.

In a *desert, <u>water</u> would be the priority* and shelter at night as it can get very cold in a desert. If the desert terrain allows, meaning not too many gullies, drop offs and crevices then it's possible to walk at night, and then do so as it's going to save water. Open sandy desert will be better for this as *mountainous desert terrain can be dangerous to travel to at night*. Sometimes the easiest things to do, such as find a spear, can be dealt with first not because they are the priority, but because they are the easiest to achieve. Such as finding a 6-foot shaft for a spear as you walk along looking for water and shelter. **So, your priorities can look something like this.**

Combine Priority Tasks

Learn to accomplish your goals simultaneously where possible e.g. as you go about looking for firewood also look for water and shelter. You can collect wood for shelter and fire at the same time **if you don't already have a shelter sheet**/parachute cord /ground sheet (plastic sheet) tent etc. Simultaneously you can look for *tinder* for fire, animals, or human spoor (animal spoor sometimes leads to water, human spoor can be a threat if you are in a military context). You might come across some very dry and flammable tinder then take some and keep it for later, if you already have some tinder add to it or take some to replenish your supply so you have more than enough, because where you are going there might be none.

NB You should learn as much as you can before you need your skills in a survival situation. You don't need to be a survival expert, but *it does help to have the basic skills such as fire*, water collection and purification, gathering food, and shelter construction. These are the basics and should be learned before anything else as they will keep you alive most consistently.

Spear

I would think a *weapon* such as a spear ***would be a priority*** as it will keep you alive, then because you are still alive you can build a shelter then look for water. Some shelters can be as simple as a tree, cave, fallen tree, but water will take some effort if there is no stream or river close by.

If you find yourself in an open savannah, then you might need to wait till you reach some trees otherwise you should have no difficulty finding a spear. Don't settle for a dried weak and bent piece of wood because this won't help if you need to use it against large animals such as leopards. It needs to be strong, resilient (slightly flexible) and at least **6 feet** 7 feet and as <u>**straight as possible,**</u> this is to take the pressure of **extreme use in a combat** situation where life or death is a potential outcome.

Water

Water is very important because you can always live without food for at least a week or two or even more and not suffer too much. <u>**You will feel lethargic**</u> after a few days and this might affect your ability to collect food, **set traps and make shelter**, so do the things that you need to ***before you get too weak to do so***. This is especially important if you think you might be there for a month or 2 because you don't want to be too weak to find the food. But if your destination is a few days walk then you will want to get there, and not spend too much time making complicated traps that will keep you in harm's way longer.

The need for water:

a. rehydrates you
b. cleans out toxins from your body as you urinate
c. keeps you warm by allowing good blood flow and the ability to drink a warm beverage
d. keeps you cool in hot weather by sweating and latent heat is given off on your skin
e. allows proper function of the muscles and metabolism (with salt can prevent cramping)
f. aids cooking (soups, stews, broth etc.)
g. allows you to wash and ***maintain a good <u>hygienic environment</u>***.

Boiling water using stones with wooden tongs:

Boiling water the traditional way:

Boiling water and tea in an improvised pottery pot:

Boiling water in bamboo:

Shelter

If it's close to dark, you had probably best find a **shelter** otherwise you might be sleeping in the open, not good if you are in an ***African savannah as the <u>predator's hunt at night</u>***. While you look for shelter you can look for your **spear** and find some **water at the same time**.

Air supply in the shelter

Don't insulate yourself in your shelter to the extent you suffocate in it, it's better to leave a small opening, even if it is cold, to allow a little air flow so you can breathe oxygen – ***it's like wearing a mask the whole day and then wondering why you are sick***, it's because you are breathing too much carbon dioxide and not enough life preserving oxygen.

Small shelters

A **small shelter** heats up quicker so keep it small and well insulated, especially the thick under cover layer such as leaves or pine needles on the ground. You first want to clear the area to search for scorpions (especially in African desert there are lots of scorpions which are dangerous but can be eaten).

a. Soft materials such as leaves are good.
b. Grass can be good but in Africa that's where ticks gather so make sure you check before use.
c. Moss (if it's not damp). There is not a lot of this in Africa but if you do come across some then it's usable for soft bedding.
d. Pine needles are best covered with a ground sheet so that the needles don't stick into you at night when you are trying to sleep. They give you an inflated section between **you and the ground.**

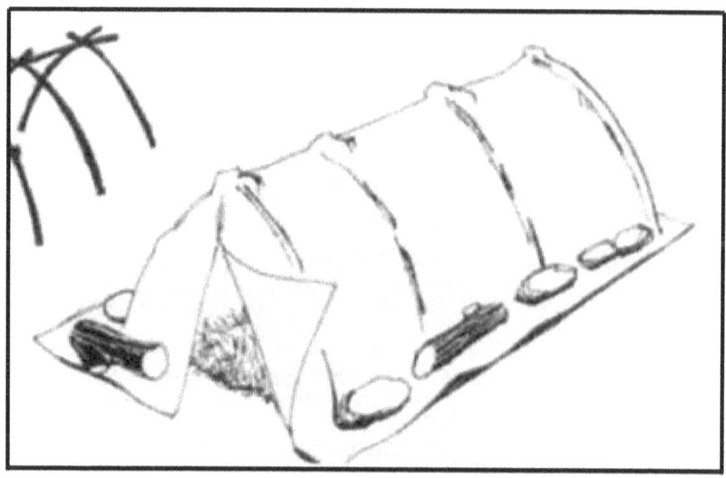

Large shelters

Large shelter can be for longer term survival e.g., a wood cabin or hut made with mud and poles with thorn bushes. This could have a large supply of wood as this is a of primary importance in a survival situation as it can be used with fire to boil water and provide warmth.

Quick, simple shelter

This is for shelter from sun/rain/wind. This is where you can make your weapon (spear/bow), traps, drink water with purifying straw, read your map and *plan your next move,* clean your gun etc. Wind chill can be devastating and can even kill you as your body temperature can fall drastically because of it. A rain or sun shelter can be a plain tarp that is suspended above you.

Fire

Because you will need to keep warm and keep predators at bay you will need to keep a look out for some tinder for your **fire,** you might have some fire-making equipment on you, and if you are prepared you will have fire steel as well as a lighter. Keep in mind **a spear** will also make a **good walking stick to keep your balance** on steep mountain paths. If you don't find a weapon then shelter is your next priority, seek fire making birds nest (fine grass), then water in the morning, spear, and food next. The main point is to **think develop a basic plan** and be aware of your surroundings.

If you found yourself in a jungle environment, you will need to **find** <u>dry tinder</u> and remember that the light goes out quickly in a jungle, so it gets dark in a few minutes. Don't get caught without a fire, *dry the tinder against your body if needed*. A fire with a **piece of an ant hill** on top makes smoke that keeps mosquitoes at bay. You will also need a shelter to keep the night showers off your fire, as the rain will put your fire out, it will take you an hour to get your fire going so you don't want it going out. Hopefully, you have at least a small knife (as your EDC) and even better if you have a large one as this will help you to build shelters, make fires, skin game, make traps etc.

Benefits of fire:

a. fire purifies water
b. cooks' food
c. keeps you warm
d. keeps wild animals away
e. gives light (can give you away in a combat survival situation)
f. good moral booster (lift your spirits)
g. 3 fires in a triangle are used as an emergency signal,

therefore signal fires are important for indicating your presence.

Food

You need food to help keep you warm/recover from injury and exertion/energy for hunting and other daily chores, replenish energy stores in the muscles.

a. Food gives you vitamins, minerals, protein, carbohydrates, and fat.
b. Food is needed for your body's ability to make heat to keep you warm.
c. Food is needed for repairing of muscles and tendons.
d. Just general wellbeing takes a certain number of calories; for a man 2500 calories and for a woman 1500-1800 calories. This is a modern estimation. The calories would have been less a few hundred years ago as people moved through the country where no shops or malls were, and people would fast (go without food for at least 3-4 weeks). Fasting is only possible if you have enough energy stores for the period and is not applicable for people that are already at 2-4 percent body fat.
e. You will in most situations only find enough food to sustain you. But don't worry about this – as mentioned you can go without food for quite a while.

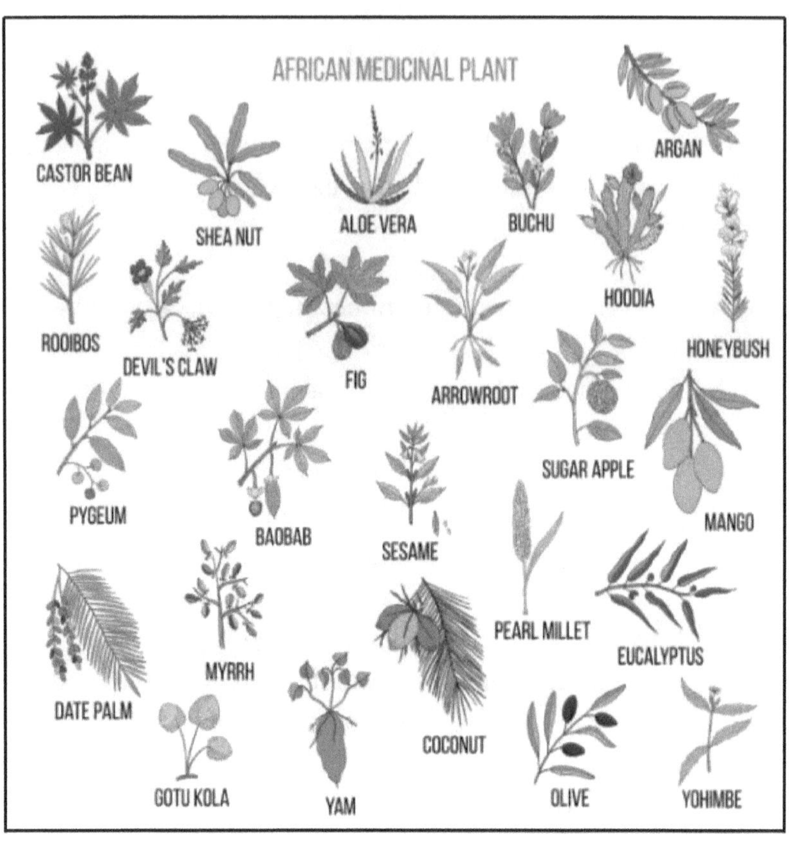

AFRICAN MEDICINAL PLANT
CASTOR BEAN
SHEA NUT
ALOE VERA
BUCHU
ARGAN
HOODIA
ROOIBOS
DEVIL'S CLAW
FIG
ARROWROOT
HONEYBUSH
PYGEUM
BAOBAB
SESAME
SUGAR APPLE
MANGO
DATE PALM
MYRRH
COCONUT
PEARL MILLET
EUCALYPTUS
GOTU KOLA
YAM
OLIVE
YOHIMBE

Equipment Requirements for Survival

Your equipment should have the following characteristics:

1. **Practical**. Your equipment must be reliable and robust, looking good is not the point, just functionality. It must be functional and strong with **utility in mind,** not fancy or looking shiny and nice. If you look at the bow, arrows, and other equipment of the Bushmen you will see that they are basic and not very sophisticated, but they are functional.

2. **Reliability**. Most **mil spec** (military specification) equipment will have been tested so this can be a guideline but still do your own testing. *You don't want your equipment breaking down on you in the field* in a survival situation. If you are already in a stressful situation the last thing you need is e.g., a blade to break when you are trying to make a fire. You might be hunting and the firing pin in your firearm breaks, this means no meat for a while. The robustness of your weapon system is important. It would be even worse if you were in a firefight and your weapon broke.

3. **Robust**. It must not break readily especially something as important as your blade. Think about something that can easily tear such as your Bivy bag which is your sleep system – if it does not keep you warm you could die. Lack of sleep leads to fatigue and fatigue to mistakes, so good sleep is important. This can exacerbate the situation if you are trying to do something such as make a fire or make a trap that requires finding motor skills.

4. The piece of equipment must **preferably** have **three or more uses**, though this is not always possible as a radio can mostly only be used to talk to someone over a distance, but

the batteries can be used to make fire. Wireless radio allows you to have a bit of news from the outside world if there is any news to be had. For example, if you have a magnifying glass then you can make fire, look for a splinter, examine a wound, read fine print, and save your matches and other fire making equipment when you are out for extended periods. Another example is rope, which has many uses including making shelter, hanging stuff from trees, making traps to catch game, etc.

5. ***It is the attitude of acquiring equipment over time that helps to achieve a few different tasks***, such as an axe that is used to chop trees or the back of the axe used for hitting nails. An example would be a magnifying glass that can be used to take splinters out, it can also make fire and used to inspect tracks (spoor) or a potential plant for food. So, it has more than one use and can therefore be considered a valuable piece of kit. The patience and determination to acquire the best equipment is what makes the difference between a person that survives or a person that dies when trouble arises.

6. ***Have the best you can buy*** in the most **important survival necessities** such as water cleaning, food acquiring, and fire. **Have at least three ways** of obtaining and cleaning water and cooking food.

a. Fire: have a lighter (it is the quickest way to start a fire), **fire steel**, *magnifying glass* and either carry tinder or look for it in the bush, it should be dry and exceptionally fine, so it catches alight easily.

b. Water carrying: Hard stainless steel water bottle/or plastic (nontoxic), water carrier bag such as Camel Back hydration pack, condoms in emergency kit. These are especially important and should be bought with *durability* and *strength* in mind.

c.   Hunting: Spear point, arrow point, ammo (22LR caliber), wire for snares, fishhooks for catching fish, netting to catch fish crabs etc.

d.   Shelter: Sleeping bag, Bivy bag to cover the sleeping bag, ground sheet, emergency plastic bags (heavy duty), shelter sheet for overhead shelter. These must be of the *highest quality and best you can buy* as this will keep you alive. As you sleep more comfortably, this will lead to better focus.

1.   **<u>Test all equipment</u>**, this was mentioned before but it is very important, so we say it again. If you miss this point, take a piece of equipment and end up dying because your knife broke it could be a catastrophe.

2.   Keep only the **<u>absolutely necessary equipment</u>** on you, don't take any items for **comfort** or **convenience** (except sleeping). You will make yourself **tired trying to carry a heavy pack**. This does not mean you do not train with a heavy pack. To give yourself the advantage, you *carry a heavy pack in training* so you can carry a lighter pack in an emergency.

3.   **The only comfort you need is a <u>good night's sleep</u>** so a good sleeping bag or good shelter making skills will be needed. Make sure you do not have your fire close to your sleeping bag as if this catches fire you will be burnt severely. Modern sleeping bags burn quickly and easily. Wool blankets do not, they just smolder so are a good option. Wool blankets are heavier. Warm modern sleeping bags are light but burn easy.

4.   **Always** get the **<u>lightest</u>** and **smallest** but most **<u>reliable</u>** *equipment* available but take a heavy piece of equipment if

it's reliable and strong (durable). **Durable** is especially important in a SHTF situation because you might not be able to replace the equipment if there is a situation such as civil war or SHTF.

5. Do not take a battery-operated <u>appliance</u> **<u>if you can't recharge</u>** it, unless the batteries are light and you have a lot of them, but this adds unnecessary weight which could be used for food or water. Some items such as thermal scopes will not be used often except for hunting so batteries might not be a problem. Thermal will also be used in a combat or SHTF situation so having one would be especially useful.

6. What you should do when you have all your equipment **you think you need**, is to now say *what I can do without* and *what must you have for purely for survival*? It is going to make it lighter if you keep it minimal. Your kit will be somewhere in between these two **necessities** and **desire** for comfort. Consider the terrain. When Bushmen travel, they have a small bag, bow, and a knife. This is extraordinarily little but if you have **knowledge**, it is doable.

Equipment Selection and Preparation

This is a guideline and how and when you collect your equipment is determined by your finances, abilities, experience and time.

Start collecting your kit now and this training you do with this manual will show you your equipment shortcomings. **Evaluate all equipment** before use in an operational/ survival environment, this is so you know **how it works** and **if it works** at all.

You do not need to collect your equipment now if you do not have the money; your equipment can be collected over a year or more if needed. Just as important to **collect your kit** is to go out and *use it* so you get used to the characteristics of how they are used most *efficiently*. A number of people spend 10-20 years collecting the best equipment their money can buy. This doesn't mean anything if you don't use it in some type of training environment.

Carry light loads but if you cannot carry light then get a means of transport so **you can carry heavy, or at least more for a long-term**

sustainable survival situation. A 4x4 or off-road vehicle and small well-built Caravan will set you in good stead.

That means: ***do not carry heavy equipment* if you do not have to**. If you do need to carry heavy equipment then try to *improvise a carry method* such as an ATV /electric bike/normal etc. (in military type war or SHTF you might need to steal it), off road vehicle, bicycle, cart, horse, mule, or any other means of getting your equipment to the destination. If you can, cache your unnecessary equipment and come back later and fetch it. If you can't for practical reasons, try hide it another way. There are other ways not discussed here to carry equipment but that would be a specialized piece of equipment such as a microlight or similar mode of transport. One of the best *covert fast and quiet means of transport will be an electric bike*.

Planning for Survival, SHTF, or Combat and Survival

Before you can plan on what to take or prepare for survival, *you need to know what the possible survival situation could be*. This will dictate what the possibilities for a survival situation happening are. This mindset applies to SHTF type situations or just planning a hiking trip.

The problem with planning for survival is *you never know when this event might happen* if at all so that means even with all the planning you **might still not have the needed equipment** as the event will *most probably be unexpected*.

This is where your everyday carry (EDC) equipment comes into its own. *It's the unexpected events that cause the most consternation for the survivor*, the ones that cause the most stress, but *where ingenuity comes in to play,* and using as much of your environment and equipment found in your vehicle, plane or boat is going to count.

If you were **an organized person** and walking in the wild you would have the basic survival equipment on you as this would be one of the situations when you would need to survive. The *more adventurous you are the more likely you will find yourself in a survival situation,* which is a risk you hopefully plan for.

Terrain Considerations

In some countries, like Namibia, the terrain can vary enormously, which impacts survival planning considerably. The further north you go, you'll find more grass and bushes with trees, and further south will be more desert. Close to the sea on the west coast it is very dry with sand and dunes and no vegetation – it is called the Skeleton Coast for good reason, as many ships run aground on the coast of Namibia, and over the centuries many sailors perished on reaching the parched shores.

Skeleton Coast of Namibia:

Northern Namibia:

As can be seen from the above pictures you can go from sand dunes, to desert coastline, to green trees and bushveld depending on where you travel in Namibia. In the north it gets greener, and more game are present. This means hunting is good and survival is easier if you have a way of killing game. The coastline will provide fishing and seals for hunting. The desert and savanna with bushveld will mean hunting antelope, ostriches, snakes, porcupines, aardvarks and warthogs etc. Even though some areas look sparse and without life, you will soon find out that there are even buck in the desert. The biggest ***problem is finding water*** in this type of terrain. Here you can find elephant dung and, if fresh, it will have water in it as elephants drink large quantities of water. This will have bacteria in it, though, and should not be attempted if you don't have to, especially if you lack water purification equipment. As shown elsewhere in this manual you can eat the protein in ostrich eggs and then use the empty eggshell to store water.

Desert Survival Equipment

It is taken for granted that *if you knew you were going to a desert* then you **would have at least water to drink and a way of carrying water, and ways of cleaning or purifying water**. This would be complemented with a thin *light tarpaulin* and *reflective blanket*. These are ideal for making a very cool shelter that is quick to put up and maintain. Traveling in any type of arid or desert environment without at least **5 liters of water on you** can be suicidal so carry at least a robust *25 liter* in your *vehicle where possible*.

1. **Clothing**: if you were able to prepare then *have light* (thin cotton) *light in color* and fully covering the whole body. Keep clothing loose and cover the head because 8 hours in the sun will give you serious burns. Even people that are used to the sun will feel it after a whole day.

2. **Water carriage**: for deserts you should have at least *2-3 ways of carrying water* to increase carrying capacity from 1 liter to **5 or more liters**. A 3-liter Camelback type bag (water bladder inside the bag), with a canteen and canteen cup should suffice if you know there is water in the desert area where you are operating. Make sure you know how to get to this water source and, if possible, know a secondary water source.

Note that in the South African military, our webbing would have 2 side pouches with capacity for a 2-liter water bottle each side and a 1-liter water bottle on the side at the back.

1. **Water purification**: a way to boil water and/or that you can clean water chemically. This means tin cup for boiling

and water tabs for cleaning water (iodine). The water you find in a pool will be contaminated as the local wildlife will drink there. It is therefore important to have a way to disinfect the water.

2. **Compass and GPS**: while knowing your direction with the sun and stars (e.g., Southern Cross) is basically useful, a good compass and even GPS will be a huge asset. Remember, celestial navigation is possible but full of mathematical detail, and good mariners take 15 minutes to get a ½ mile fix on their position with a sextant and lots of printed tables. Efficiency is the name of the game, so quick and accurate navigation items are ideal.

3. **Shelter**: thin light tarp with extra tarp with *reflective material for shelter (can also be used to signal). This can be made more efficient* if you can have a breeze blowing through the shelter.

Basic Survival Loadout

You may be hiking on the mountain and get injured. These situations last a *few days* to weeks but mostly a few days. *Your basic survival equipment loadout* will count here; shelter (*maintain body core temperature which is approx. 37 C*), fire (cook food/sterilize water/ keep warm), water (prevent dehydration) and food (maintain health) if you prepared properly, you have at **least 3 days' worth of food water** and gear such as fire making equipment. Then it would help if you had communications such as hand-held two-way radios, *GPS with radio capacity* (Garmin Rhino) or cell phone. *People will look for you where you said you would be in your preplanning*, as this would be part of your survival strategy. Your 3-day bag should suffice in this type of situation if properly packed.

Satellite phone:

A basic survival situation where the vehicle has broken down or you got lost in the bush or similar will be dealt with or *managed by a 3-day bag*. If a 3-day bag is **used properly (extensive knowledge)** it can sustain you for at least a 1 to 2 weeks period **depending on your skill level** (fasting is part of this time), *providing you have the*

ability to catch food and eat some wild edibles, that is if you know what they are, the wild edibles that is. If you are on your own you can spread the food that is in your bag and catch food with traps. This is because this type of scenario will normally not go longer than 14 days; here water is going to be more important. Dehydration can set in after 1-3 days and is dependent on your fitness, conditioning to heat and lack of water (the Kalahari Bushmen have very little water each day).

A survival situation can be longer in some instances, such as sea survival situations where people were at sea for 1 to 2 months, but this is very unusual. Most of the time you will only need to worry about food by the 3rd or 4th day as your body can use your fat stores. Sea survival for long periods is only possible for people that have a lifeboat and supplies with fishhooks and *water supply from evaporation and condensation* which is found in some survival kits for boats. The difference for loadout versus combat survival will be that basic survival will be just **staying alive** so these items can be carried in a 15–20-liter bag or bigger depending on mission requirements.

Use a basic small 35–45-liter survival bag with basic items and added to this a chest webbing for any added combat survival, the actual loadout is determined by <u>**the context**</u> of the situation. Having a combat loadout will be normal, when you have planned for a combat situation and where survival is part of the scenario.

The good or excellent part is having the time and ability to plan for this, which helps to survive. Having a loadout that is <u>**complete**</u> but **not too <u>heavy</u>** is ideal. Too heavy equipment is going to tire you out. Too little is going to leave you wanting more, as in not having a sleeping bag can be debilitating as **lack of sleep will tire you.** Here the very basics must suffice, such as a light compact Gortex sleeping outer. **Fire making** equipment, high quality **fixed blade**, Monocular. These are examples but not limited to these items as different circumstances will dictate other items such as water carrying bags for desert areas. Here 2 water bottles and two 1-liter plastic foldable water containers will be of absolute importance. For dessert you might also consider a reflective tarp to reflect heat away during day and reflect heat towards you at night.

This doesn't mean you do not plan to have another bag with more essentials and maybe even a large 3rd bag superficially for food.

Example of a heavy-duty tarp with reflective material:

The vest and chest webbing that you use will function as an excellent light but comprehensive loadout for general purposes whether SHTF, civil war or general unrest. This is light enough to be combat effective and comprehensive enough to be used for survival even though only **very basic equipment can be carried in a 20–30-liter bag**. The light color of the bag also allows it to be camouflaged if you feel this is appropriate for the type of situation you find yourself in.

This should always be an option for any type of SHTF/civil unrest type scenario.

Small bag (day bag can be 20-30 liter) for food and water, warm clothes, and **chest webbing** for combat related equipment:

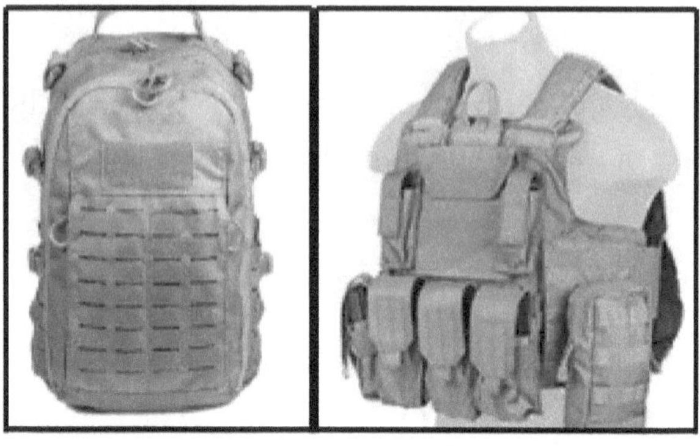

This assault vest will
suffice for combat
supplies and
some survival items

Natural Disaster Loadout

Natural disasters could take a long time to resolve and or for government to deal with and evacuation to occur therefore government help/assistance may take weeks. This type of survival situation will be a longer survival period. This means having sufficient food stocks (and rifles and ammunition for those countries where civilians can acquire such).

1. This situation can be anything from weeks to months for everything to normalize but you will not stay in the area if there is combat (war or SHTF/WROL) Therefore you will need enough supplies to get to a safe town/city/venue. This means supplies that will last till you either **get to a cache** of ammunition water and food or till you reach the designated haven. This depends on the distance and time it takes to travel to your destination, which could be 2 days to 2 weeks if on foot. Therefore, food for 2 days does not need to be more than a *few pieces of biltong* (jerky) and some *carbohydrate such as rolled oats* or '2 minute' noodles for emergency. Just eat healthy food once you're at your designated location.

2. For longer term survival such as 2 weeks you will need 500g - 1kg biltong and 1kg oats with some multivitamin tablets. Keep in mind *the body can quite easily deal with a week without food.* **Water will be vital** as *your performance will diminish very quickly after a day without water.* Floods or earthquakes can cause water shortages and electricity and related infrastructure failure e.g., the Fukushima nuclear power plant in Japan was damaged by a tsunami which in turn caused contamination which was a risk for people in the area. It seems to have

also affected the ocean area around Fukushima.

3. These events can take weeks or months to fix so expect anything from 2 weeks to a few months for things to normalize in a natural disaster. Planning for this time means months' worth of food and water. <u>**Ideally**</u> you also have the means *of self-defense* as this will be relevant in the first or second week of any disaster as people will be desperate. ***Very few people expect a natural disaster*** and that is why it is a life threating situation. This situation will be in part due to lack of food, water, and **hygiene items**, which were not accumulated for such occasions, thus illustrating the concept that "failing to plan is planning to fail."

Civil Unrest Loadout

Civil unrest will be a difficult situation to plan for as it can take days to months to subside. There is an extra consideration or dimension in this type of survival situation. One dimension is your survival items such as food and shelter etc. and the *second is combat and evasion of violent gangs or enemy troops* (depending on the scenario). These are the considerations for that type of survival e.g., finding **food, water, and shelter** as well as the <u>security concern</u>. It is safe to say that in a civil unrest type scenario you could be surviving for months, even a year or more. If you shelter in place (at home) you will have most of your supplies, the time duration will put strain on your **organization** such as food, ammunition, water, *broken components of your transport or weapon systems*. But you will have an increased security situation being at home with ammunition and food as time progresses, things might get better or worse depending on the government's planning. This is dependent on what type and the reason for the unrest. As we see now in frequent news reports, a few *hundred strikers (hooligans) can incapacitate the transport of food to distribution* areas where this has taken place. In some cases, gasoline/petrol might be limited and hard to find and even non-existent. This is why food, equipment, transport, and fuel must be stored up and this has to be done over a period that allows you to get enough of your stores needed for survival. This is more of a political type of survival scenario than finding yourself alone and stuck in the middle of nowhere.

Civil Unrest Planning and Operations

1. Civil unrest is one of the hardest situations to plan for. This is especially relevant *when having to be moving on foot and with limited supplies*. This is because you can (depending on your fitness level and strength including muscle endurance) only *carry 2-3 weeks at max of food* in a pack and water for a couple of days then you will need to resupply from a place where stores are (friends / fellow prepares / caches / government stores if it was a SHTF situation etc.). Survival in this scenario is only viable if the scenario was *planned for with supply caches spread over the distance* of your route as insurance for problems in your area. This is if you have planned for such a scenario beforehand and have the forethought and insight into your country's situation that you can plan such a **supply cache chain in direction of your destination.** A survival cache is a long-term survival strategy and is appropriate if you feel this is appropriate in your country. This does not affect our survival in a standard survival situation where you get stranded or lost.

2. You will need to **consider *your route*** which would be dictated by security concerns and *cache locations*, marked on your map (landmarks kept in your head) for **combat survival**. The route you choose should have aspects of **cover** and **concealment (bush or forest)** along the way, if possible, some resting up places (also referred to as LUP's or laying up place) if you are walking for a few days then this will be especially relevant. Make use of and look for any **natural cover** to sleep in like caves or under treefalls etc. One reason to search for an expedient cover is that an *expedient shelter* is better than spending 4 hours making a

shelter. This is to save energy and time, and this is to your advantage, *because it is* **efficient**. This time saved by an expedient shelter leaves more energy for important tasks like cleaning your weapon and eating to build up your energy levels.

3. It also means you have more time where you can observe the route you took into the Hide (LUP) when using the hook method of walking past then doubling back to your hide. You should in some circumstances **apply all anti tracking techniques and camouflage** discipline if the situation warrants it (SHTF) you could call this your SOP. This means when entering and exiting your hide, covering your tracks will be important, this means choosing terrain that minimizes your sign. This is especially relevant when you are going to use your resting up place for a few days.

4. The map below is an idea of what a map will look like on a 1:50 000 with caches and places of shelter with reason for choosing them in your notes. This could be cover and concealment, for water (this will be especially important), a **high point for observation** over the hunting area etc. The map shown is only an example, not how you lay out a map. An actual map would have more detail and more stops, with more caches if you are traveling more than 50 or 60km. Each 10mm is 1 km and using a printed **1:50 000 map will typically mean an area about 25 km wide**. So, if your place of refuge is in the middle of the map you have about 12km of detail surrounding that.

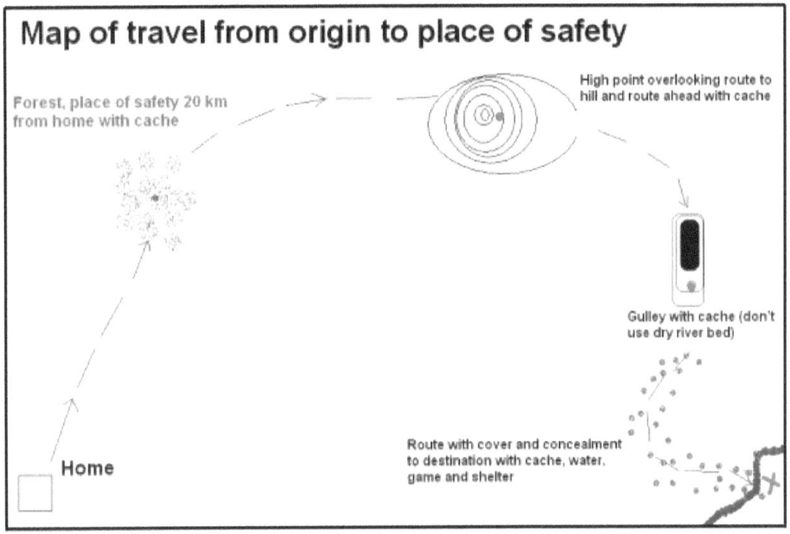

1. Your **dress** will be **dictated by the severity** of the situation and needs of the operator or survivor such as either blending in when in an urban environment by using same dress as the locals, or using camouflage out in the rural areas that is appropriate to the area you find yourself in. Desert will be different to jungle. Use **camouflage** if you know the **area is hostile** to people traveling through and consider low profile dress such as colors that blend with the environment e.g., soft browns- and grass-colored fabrics (coyote brown/kaki) but are not necessarily obvious camouflage patterns (as military type camouflage can draw unwanted attention to you). You might as well use actual camouflage patterning if you are walking through an area in a combat or civil unrest situation as you will already draw attention to yourself if you are carrying a weapon for self-defense, though *this should be concealed, if possible,* especially if you are in an urban environment. Out of

urban and in the wild it will not matter to carry concealed.

2. Dress according to the combat environment or survival scenario. It is not unusual for people to wear camouflage so it's not a big deal in most people's minds **unless it's full camouflage from head to toe** with maybe a veil, as that would stick out. Not so much a camo jacket. If you want to be more covert but want to be able to convert to full camo then wear **camo pants** and then just add jacket and head dress when you transition to a bush environment.

This picture below on the left would be more appropriate to a SHTF situation and the second picture below would fit in to a normal survival situation where concealment is not important:

Compass
Spare mags
Belt webbing
Pistol
Integrated leg pads

Combat survival clothing:

Normal survival clothing:

1. *Your time of movement*, which refers to the early morning
   or *late evening movement*, is important as well, and *the
   route you will take* might be restricted by unrest and
   chaos. Normal survival situations such as a vehicle
   breakdown will need planning **for days** of survival and
   civil unrest might mean planning for <u>weeks and months</u>.
   As a rough guideline a normal situation that is a survival
   scenario will be any time of day or night for movement if
   you do not have to worry about assailants (attackers). You
   do not have to worry about opponents /assailants as
   mentioned therefore your movement can be at any time. In
   a combat/SHTF environment you will find it safer to
   move between 12:00 in the evening (24:00) to 05:00 in

morning. If it is a *real combat situation* (war) then you might want to move between *03:00 in the morning till 05:00 in the morning*.

2. Another crucial point is to sit down and *first work out <u>what you want to prepare for,</u>* then **decide what you need**. Realistically we can see that some situations only require a few days of supplies. Complex scenarios require a few months of supplies and more intensive planning with regards to **location** and **logistics**. Locations such as desert regions will dictate you have more water and food. This will also be dictated by and involved with your **movement** by vehicle or foot and time to move, do you have to move immediately or do you have 1-2 weeks to prepare. This will be logistics such as fuel, water, food, batteries, shelter and sleeping bags as an example.

Speak to people with and experience as there is no teacher like genuine experience. *Keep your plans simple* but **consider the entirety of your location and its challenges**, such as **Africa which is more dangerous than most continents** due to the **wildlife** and indigenous **populations which can be extremely dangerous**. This is different for people that live in Europe or some Middle Eastern countries, some areas in US, most European countries where it is only the population that is dangerous and not so much the terrain (if not a desert/snow) or animals. Each country will have its own challenges and tests. This is only going to be known by people with **specific expertise in the local environment**.

This is why making a survival manual that includes all region-specific scenarios or challenges is almost impossible. *Applying general survival concepts should be taught or described* and then *specifics can be illustrated and described for a specific continent such as Africa*, but as for applying all concepts, techniques and tactics would not be possible. If we consider that the edible plants species may be numerous and this would or should also include poisonous plants as these could end your survival situation quickly. This does not include the specifics challenges experienced by the region's weather and terrain such as flat dry landscapes or mountains as both will have their own challenges and will cause you to equip and plan for survival in that environment **specific to that terrain.**

So, **plan according to your area of operations**, if it is a desert environment plan for a lot of water and *know* all the *wells/rivers* and other water sources. Plan on a map if you have a map as this might be more for planning for SHTF as you might not have a map when being stranded.

Survival Equipment

Blades

A big blade will save you time and energy but it is harder to carry in the open in an urban environment if you are trying to be covert. They also serve many purposes and are easy to carry in the bush – on your hip or attached to your bag. With this you can carry a small, fixed blade for cutting rope or making traps. This does not have to be a fixed blade, but if it is a folder, it must be ***exceptionally durable***. Make sure it cannot fall out and that **the sheath** is durable and has at least a **double retention** system. Examples are given in this manual of some large and small survival blades.

Knife

You'll need to *carry a fixed blade* on you in the first place to make items, build fires and fashion a bow or spear. If nothing else at least a very sturdy folding blade, but *preferably a fixed blade with full tang*. This is because a fixed blade is less likely to break, and a broken blade is almost useless. You could still improvise a spear from the broken blade, but this is only if the blade did not break in the middle. The knife will allow you to fashion a *throwing stick* that can be thrown by the survivalist to kill a bird or rabbit or other small game. This is technically easier to find and use than a spear, but a spear is very deadly and a particularly good hunting tool.

The blade will allow you to make snares, cut wood for a shelter or for a fire. <u>**Efficiency** </u> **is the name of the game,** and you should **spend as little effort as possible for the most food, water, shelter,** and **fire.** Make the fire **properly the first time** and take your time with all the *elements to make the fire*, which is **fuel** (wood tinder) fuel to start which is any material that is highly flammable (cotton wool, fine steel wool, char cloth, pine resin mixed with cat tails), **oxygen** (enough air) and a **spark or flame**, sun energy (magnifying glass), friction or chemical.

Therefore, processing firewood, making shelter or making animal traps are all functions that are made easier or possible with a sturdy knife. A larger knife such as a **Kukri or Parang** will make large chopping tasks easier, and it is therefore a *blessing to have one*. Even though this might not be possible in a survival situation as these emergencies happen when you least expect it.

Small survival knife with sheath and survival items: this is my personal survival knife, and it has everything in it to survive in a basic situation, it's a solid but small blade for the general task of survival:

A good knife and pouch (sheath) contain the following items for general and emergency use. This covers direction finding, fire, fishing, paracord for shelter and traps. Fire for warmth and signaling for help. Fishing line can be used to sew up a minor cut after you have washed it out. You can add a condom to this as a water carrying capacity:

1. Fixed blade knife
2. Cord: 550 paracord
3. Magnetized needle for direction finding and sowing
4. Fishhooks
5. Nylon for fishing hooks
6. Fire steel for fire
7. Cotton wool with petroleum jelly as tinder
8. Emery (sandpaper) for sharpening your knife

Small fixed blade

Do not let it fall out of your pocket. Make sure it has a **good retention clip**, sheath, or holder and or lanyard tied to your pants loops and inserted into the pocket or ***tied on to the belt while in the sheath***.

See picture below for context where teaspoon is for size comparison. This is just an option not what you should carry. The large blade is for e.g., chopping through thick bush and the small one for smaller tasks around camp etc.:

Folding blade

The 'folder' must be durable, or it will not last in a survival situation. The locking system must be extraordinarily strong, so you don't injure yourself. The size is not that important as you will only use it for camp tasks such as cutting twine or cord, making a trap, witling, or other basic tasks. This can even be a ridiculously cheap blade but don't forget it must lock properly and be strong enough to not break easily.

My carry option Cold Steel xx voyager made in Japan:

Large blade

A large blade should always be part of your equipment because it has so many uses and can make life much easier if you have one, it can double as a **carving tool** and **chopping tool** and **self-defense** tool, small knives use a lot of energy to make a shelter. You can baton a piece of wood, but it takes a lot of energy if you don't know how.

Collection of potential survival knives: cheaper option will be this cold steel Kukri; these will do the job and cover you (not excellent steel but can do the job):

Smith and Wesson large survival knife: Classic US Marine K-bar:

Large Bowie 8-inch style knife for general survival – it's not good for small tasks, only hacking and such tasks (also good for fighting):

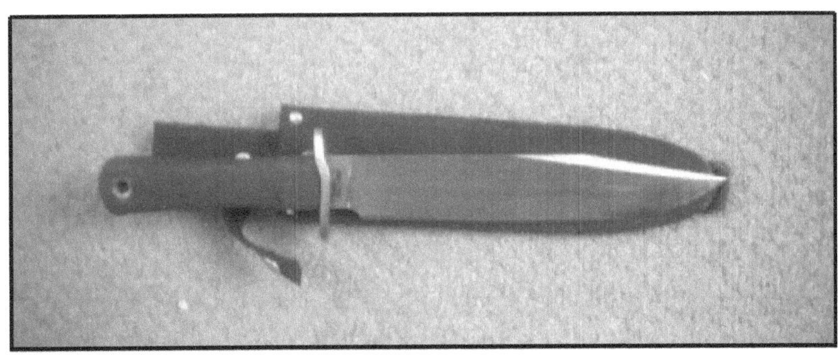

Large 12-inch blade for chopping:

Axes

Axes are heavy and are only good for chopping wood. They take a lot of energy like a big blade but are not as good for fighting with as a big blade is. This is unless the axe is a ***light fighting tomahawk***, then it might be ***useful to use for fighting***. But a light tomahawk is not good for chopping wood, so it is a tossup between what you find most important. Even though the tomahawk is not ideal for chopping because the blade is very thin as can be seen in the picture below, it can chop a tree of about forearm thickness in about 30 minutes depending on your strength and fitness.

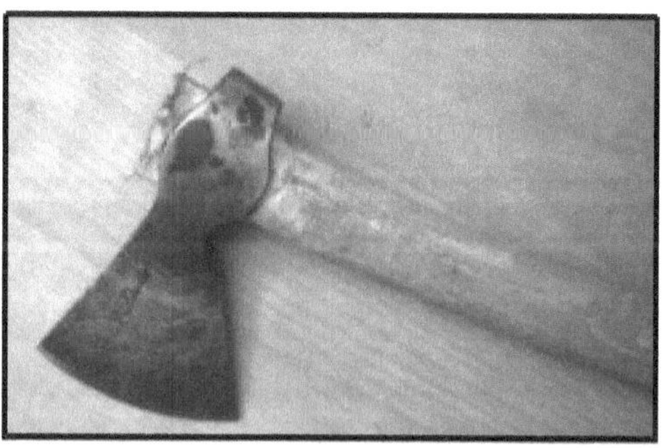

Saws

Handheld collapsible saws are great as they can be light and easy to carry and use less energy than hacking at a tree with an axe or blade. ***Remember the principle of efficiency***. They come in many qualities and strengths, you will need to choose one that suits your needs when it comes to weight and size, and manufacture quality will dictate its longevity.

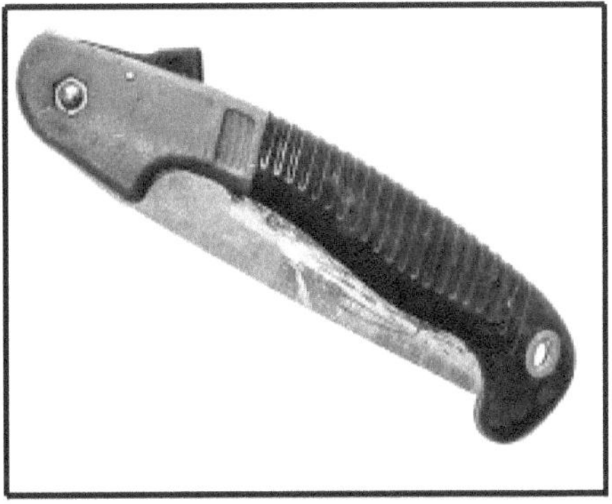

Pruning clippers

Pruning clippers can be used for hides and cutting away small bushes but you will have to decide whether it is worth taking along for the usefulness it affords. As always, make sure they're robust and strong enough for the task. This item can be used when entering a small bush to make a temporary hide (Observation Post) for hunting or surveillance.

Wire saws

Wire saws are light and easy to carry and are a useful tool for your **emergency survival kit**, be aware that ***some*** are heavy and robust and won't fit too easily into a small survival kit. Some wire saws are small, light, *flimsy* and will ***break easily*** so test it first and ***don't rely on anything flimsy for real survival***. From my experience the cheap ones that you find at most camping stores are **very flimsy** and are not robust enough for proper survival equipment.

Spade

Spades are important for some survival situations and for military use but are not as essential for normal "stuck in the bush" survival type situations. Test that the spade that you choose is robust and does not break when you dig as you would have carried a heavy piece of equipment for nothing. Failure of this tool will be both irritating and life threatening if you are digging a *fox hole for fighting.*

Weapons

These are a few weapons to consider and the first 3 will stand you in good stead to catch food and defend yourself from predators. Keep in mind *the more prepared* you are before going into any situation, whether everyday driving around in town every day during work or traveling to some campsite, *the less you need to worry*. You can have a small backpack with all the essentials in. That is unless you live in South Africa as your car will likely be stolen within a short period of time.

Spear

This is the easiest to obtain. The spear head should either be in your survival E&E bag, or you will need to make one. The quickest way to make one is to have a blade that fits the profile of a spear in your survival kit. Companies make throwing knives that are cheap and can be converted to a spear point quiet easily.

When you walk in your area that you are stranded in, especially if it is an African context, the **survival priority** should be **make a weapon**. Simple weapons are the best options initially. This is because most dangerous animals are on the African plains. The best weapon for an African environment is **initially** a *spear* as it is easy to make if you have a *spear point in your vehicle/backpack* as part of your preparedness or EDC everyday carry. You will be very efficient in hunting as they are deadly if used properly, and with skill can be thrown far with accuracy.

This is also an *excellent self-defense* weapon and has been used for 4 500 years since Noah's flood. Having basic use or skills with a spear can be learnt quickly and it is a fearsome weapon against man and animal. A bow would be good if time and expertise were available to make one. The Kalahari Bushmen survive with a spear and knife so that is possible for you if you have the expertise.

Survival spear:

Bow

The next best weapon if the survival situation that was prolonged would be a **bow and arrow**. The time taken to make and learn its characteristics will mean the situation will be weeks or months. This is only viable if the game is **plentiful, and time** is available to learn the bow and hunt. This has also been used to great effect since Noah's time (**4500 years ago**. Once again this is a very deadly weapon and can be used up to 20-30 meters depending on your skill level, if the bow is well made from a good wood that is strong and flexible.

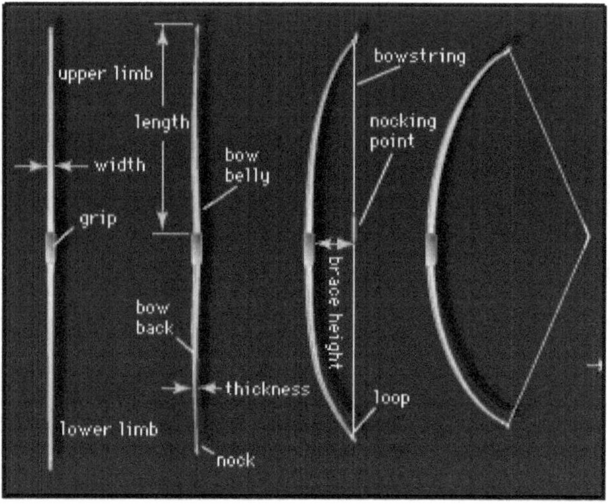

The bow is deadly and does not need to be a very strong bow to kill a small game animal at 10-15 meters. If you look at the **Bushmen** bow it is very small and weak, but the *arrow poison* helps to incapacitate the animal. A small recurve and compact bow such as the type of bow that the Mongols used, was short and powerful. This bow is **very difficult to make** and is only practical in a situation that is prolonged, and you have the skill to make one. Then if possible if the wood is available and the expertise is available and the skills to make a long bow such as used by the English in 15th century when hunting large game would be possible if you had the expertise.

You will need good string 550 cord or the inner strands of the 550 inner strands, sinew or some other strong cord made from plants such as Sansevieria. This plant can also be used for antiseptic purposes as well.

Club

The next weapon could be a ***bludgeoning weapon*** that can be used to dispatch the quarry (this would be called a knopkierie in Afrikaans and "knobkierie" in South African English), commonly known as a ***club*** or ***truncheon***. Again, this can be made with a good blade.

A club is easy to find, this is only for close range use for dispatching animals. It can be thrown, used as a backup when hunting with the bow as it's very easy to wound an animal. It can also be used when hunting at a hole where an animal has a burrow, such as a warthog.

Firearm

A weapon for survival such as a ***22LR caliber rifle*** is a fantastic tool but the chances you will have such a tool for survival is unlikely as it is harder to carry around than a large blade. In a long-term survival situation, you want something like a 22LR rifle/pistol as it will make life much easier, ammo is easy to carry, and some survival rifles only weigh 500g-1500g. Sound "suppressed" barrels (also called "silencers") are best as you do not want to scare the local wildlife away from your area of operations.

Suppressed 22LR pistol:

The Navy Seals and other SF units used to carry a suppressed 22LR/ or 9mm pistol, affectionately called a 'hush puppy' by the Seals. Otherwise for personal defense a 9mm pistol with fifteen round magazine capacity and 4 spare magazines will do. The above is an example of a suppressed 22LR pistol which is ideal for hunting small game and in an emergency for self-defense, keep in mind the shot placement will have to be perfect given the lower power of the cartridge.

The situation will determine what type of weapon you should carry; if the situation is out of control, then a rifle in 22LR or 223 is best. Semi auto high capacity is best for all round defense and hunting small game. Although the 223 calibers with good hunting bullet heads will be good for medium to small game such as a springbok, duiker and steenbok. Keep in mind in dire situations you can even use a 9mm for hunting small game, the problem is to be effective you need to be within about twenty-five meters of the game. Here shot placement will also be important as if the bullet strikes a bone, then the 9mm bullet will not be powerful enough to penetrate. A suppressed carbine such as a compact 9mm with an ***8-inch barrel*** will add ***velocity*** and ***accuracy*** to your hunting capabilities and you could use your side arm as a backup.

Throwing stick

Throwing stick and spear are best, don't just have a throwing stick, you can put the animal down quickly with a spear, this is expedient because wild animals can also wound or injure you when they have been injured and are not incapacitated.

Sling

Takes a lot of practice to use but is deadly if you know how to use it. The impracticality of this weapon is the use of it means you need practice, and this is not always possible in a quick or short duration survival scenario.

Catapult

A catapult can be very accurate if you know how to use it and are willing to do a little practice with it. The catapult can also be **used with an arrow** that you use with a ring placed in the middle of the catapult. This is very deadly if you use an arrow. Be careful when you use it – you will either injure or kill someone if the arrow hits them accidently or on purpose.

Fire Starting Equipment

Fire starting can be achieved by friction, but it is much easier to carry **fire steel** or something like fire steel, such as a blast match. **Carry the fire steel in your pocket** and one in your backpack. There are several ways to make a fire with stuff around you (e.g., birch bark in US, Asia, and Europe).

The easiest way to start a fire is using a **lighter**. This can be *any reliable lighter* such as fire steel and striker or fire steel with blade, magnesium with striker (basically a type of magnesium tinder connected to the striker which creates the spark).

Remember any fire making is made easier with <u>**good tinder**</u> (very flammable material) this can be steel wool (used with battery)/cotton wool and Vaseline/ powdered bark/pine tree shavings (thin)/cotton wool soaked in alcohol and for effect Vaseline as well etc. Other ways of making fire are discussed in other sections of the manual but you should train and experiment and do <u>**some research**</u>. **You will produce or find other pieces of equipment that might suit you better.** It is much easier to use some technology to get a fire going but if you do not have any items to get a fire going then you need to know the friction method which requires skill and training as well as the right type of wood.

Water Carriage

1. **Water <u>carrying</u> containers**/bags: these can come in many shapes, materials, and sizes but they should have at least a 1-liter capacity. If possible, you can carry **extra water carrying foldable bags** made from tough plastics for times when you will be far from a water source and traveling. This means two bags that have a capacity of 2-3 liters, **not full of water but as an extra capacity** when needed. They can be tucked in the side pockets of your backpack till needed. Always keep in mind **extra equipment can be buried** if needed.

   a. If possible, combine water carrying with cooking. That means a ***stainless steel one liter water bottle*** for carrying and boiling water (soup/stew), or something like an 'army' water bottle which is plastic with a metal cup that is one unit carried in durable heavy cotton webbing. This is best for 'belt carry' when only carrying this and a survival kit.

   b. Plastic bags or condoms can serve as ***emergency water carrying*** capacity so carrying plastic bags that carry about 1liter is a clever idea as they take up little space and increase your water capacity by 1-2 liters. Do not fill a condom with more than 1 liter of water. Normally you will need to put the condom in a sock or similar container to stop it from bursting.

   c. **Water bladder**: when you look for water carrying bags (water bladder such as Camel Back products) don't skimp on the cost as the make will determine how much of a plastic taste and toxins you get and how healthy (expedient) the material is to keep water in. There are a number of companies worldwide, **don't go for cheap ones**

made in China rather go for a type made in one of the 1st world countries of the West e.g., USA, Germany, France, Australia, UK.

Water Filtration and Purification

Improvised water filters using stones, gravel, sand, and charcoal in layers, with cloth placed at the neck so that the gravel doesn't get into your clean water.

Pebbles
Sand
Charcoal
Sand
Gravel
Twigs

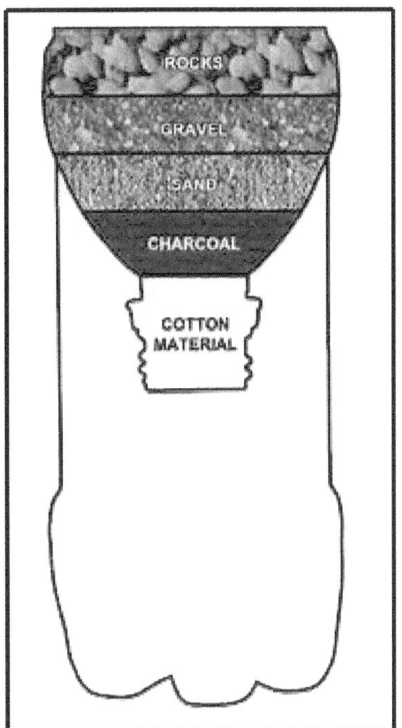

Water purification is a matter of experience, expertise, and personal preference but we discuss the types of water purification below. One of the aspects we did not discuss below is carrying a small device that **pumps water** through it to clean or purify it.

a. These take up space but are quick and efficient if you want to carry one in a large backpack. Another device which comes in handy is the drinking and ***purifying*** **straw** designed to be small and compact yet allows you to clean water quickly and efficiently without too much hassle. This is the most efficient and quickest method of having clean water.

b. Boiling is an option but will not be very efficient in a combat situation, this is because ***smoke can be seen and*** *smelt for miles* so this will give your position away and make it difficult to conceal your position. Keep in mind a small Dakota fire will give off less smoke and smell so use this when needed.

c. Chemical purification such as those with silver in can work but if you need water immediately then it is better to use a filter straw (survival straw), as chemical purification can take 30 min to 1 hour. This is especially if you are running (E&E) or are in an extremely hot climate and need to rehydrate quickly then the survival straw is a good option.

d. For efficiency's sake first use a straw if this is not available then go with chemical and if this is not available then use boiling water as an option but as stated this will give you away.

Flashlight/Torch

These are about money and what is available in your country – some countries have a predominance of certain makes that are advertised or sold by the stores that sell high quality flashlights. Some examples are Surefire (very robust made in US), LED Lenser (German design), stream light [scorpion]. These are expensive but worthwhile. A **torch with a solar charger** on it will be very practical as the batteries in a survival situation will be non-existent except what you carry on you. As has been discussed before, the heavy weight of batteries will be extremely heavy and cumbersome.

Micro-LED Light

Low light torch such as a mag-light/ **micro-LED** lights/LED Lenser K1 can be used around the camp, when *looking at maps* at night, during night travel or operations, search an area for a lost item at night. These can be very handy and helpful so get one and keep it in your main bag in your small **survival bag** that is always kept on your hip when in the field when traveling or hunting and moving away from your main bag (see below).

Small LED's can be the size of a large button and be exceptionally light with about 40 hours light time so you can carry 2 or 3 if needed. This is mostly going to be used around camp, reading a map at night, or doing chores where a powerful torch will be overkill.

Headlamps

Headlamps are used when negotiating a mountain pass at night (*if no security issues* exist such as civil unrest), making camp at night, reading a map, or searching for food at night (*catching fish*). Any situation that needs hand's free function.

Many companies make these headlamps, but I would always go for a good reliable make that has a lot of light time. Remember it must be **robust**, **light,** and work under many different conditions e.g., rain, cold, heat and dust. Different makes are Surefire, LED Lenser, and Petzl.

a. This is also carried in your belt or combat webbing, or in your survival bag. This is because you need it at hand when moving at night or when needing to look for an item dropped or when tracking at night.

b. For use in a combat environment when identification is needed you will need an 80 lumens or higher headlamp, remember you can't keep the torch on as this will give your position away and people always shoot at the light so that means your enemy will shoot your head more easily.

c. Tracking animals at night can be done but keep in mind tracking a buck at night is more dangerous in Africa as predators will also be hunting at night.

d. Arriving at a camp site at night due to lack of timing or due to events unforeseen. Use the headlamp to set up your basic camp site and set up of sleeping quarters.

e. Setting game traps at night if unable to set them during day, this will be more difficult but possible.

Handheld Light

Powerful handheld torches with an immensely powerful light such as your LED Lenser are used for tactical purposes (don't use till need to ID a target, then shoot (engage target) and move). They can also be used signaling but remember such a powerful light can be seen very far off so only use if the security situation allows.

Procurement Of Food

You need equipment for procurement of food such as plants or hunting game. If it is hunting game by trapping, then it is expedient if you **do not make complicated** traps but rather *more (5-10) simple traps* to increase your potential to catch game. This will depend on how prepared you were to survive, in the first place, *if you were prepared* for your hike and had a small survival bag with essentials then you might survive. You might have put a semi auto *22LR Caliber rifle/pistol in the* bag which means you do not have to put up snares, this is going to be *a lot more efficient*.

Having small traps like rat traps can be efficient and can help but that is the professional organization of someone who really can plan for survival trapping. This is unlikely in a normal survival situation where you are **blessed** to even have a knife and some rope with flint and steel which might be part of your everyday carry (it is part of mine). Some people carry a survival tin as part of their everyday carry.

Rat trap:

Therefore, if you do not have a weapon such as a *22 Cal rifle* to *procure small game* have provisions for simple traps such as plain wire for making a noose. You can have *more traps to increase your*

chances of snaring one animal, and complicated traps might not even catch anything. ***Complicated traps also take long to build – remember, you're a survivor and not a bushman*** that stays in the environment in which you are now surviving. You do not have weeks or months to catch game or learn the finer details of your environment. **In a military environment you also want to be as <u>efficient as possible</u>** and therefore have a quick way of obtaining food using a small caliber e.g., twenty-two long rifle (22LR), pistol or rifle.

22LR weapons or even a 22 caliber pellets gun can take down all small game such as birds and rabbits:

Stove

There are several expensive options and some cheaper options. Example stoves: alcohol (left), Esbit (center), gas (right):

Esbit stove

The Esbit stove uses small fuel blocks and is light and easy to carry, this is only for quick and small stuff such as coffee, boiling some water, making a cup of soup, purifying some water. The fuel for the Esbit is small but doesn't smell very nice and shouldn't be used in a closed tent (shelter). It is easy to light.

Gas stove

The more expensive options such as gas stove are going to cook water fast and allow fast easy cooking, but you need to carry sufficient fuel canisters. There are many on the market so do research for the best one for you. Remember it doesn't take much effort to make a fire and cook on it, so a stove is a convenience in a way. You might want to use a gas stove in situations where you need a quick option that doesn't give off any or very little smell. This is especially important in combat or reconnaissance type operations.

a. They must be robust (strong *military spec is always good*)
b. light and compact (see above Esbit stove)
c. Serve the purpose you want it for, **don't carry any gear you don't need to** carry
d. Easy to use and pack in your bag, simplicity is best as any complicated stove will have more potential to break down than a simple one (not too bulky).

Gas stoves are small and light but take more room than Esbit and alcohol stoves, they need 2 cannisters to be used for a long hiking camping trip and might not last long enough in a SHTF scenario.

Alcohol stove

Alcohol stove is exceptionally light, can carry lots of fuel and is a good option. Alcohol is fairly easy to carry and the stove is very compact and very easy to use, just remember *you can't always see the flame* and can get burnt by the flame if you are unaware that it is burning.

Improvised stoves

TWO WAYS TO USE
No Need to Bring Liquid Fuel Canisters
SOLIDIFIED ALCOHOL
LEAVES DRIED TWIGS WOOD, ETC

Radios

Radios are a convenience in a normal survival situation but are **essential in a <u>tactical</u>** (military/ security) situation. It will help to have them if you are concerned about your survival in a civil unrest type situation brought on by an earthquake or flood. There are many types but the ones which give you a **long-range** capacity are the Motorola/ Icom/Uniden/Arcshell *(keep in mind I have only used Motorola and Icom, so I am not aware of the robustness of the other brands)* **UHF/VHF** radios and other similar types. For **short-range** communications that only use **FM frequency** and low power output you can use a **Motorola talk about** but don't expect long-range communications unless you are high up and you have a clear line of sight. The Uniden SX 507 -2CKHS seems to have a good range of *50 miles* (**test for yourself**) and it's waterproof. Also look at Yaesu VX-6R ham radio transceiver. I am not a radio expert so use what you find is robust and reliable for your budget.

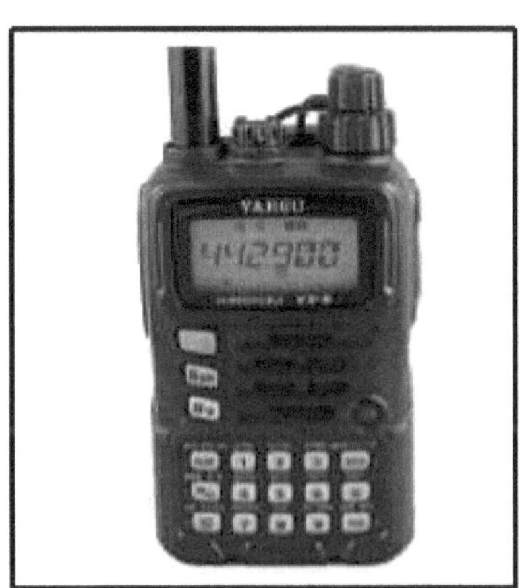

a. Your radio must be ***carried on your belt webbing***, like your weapon you can't leave it lying around or leave it in your pack unless it is a backup, or you don't need to use it with any urgency.

b. The radio must be accessible but out of the way of your security equipment (security equipment would be handgun, magazines, combat knife and other combat items).

c. Know your **<u>frequency</u>** and **channels.**

d. Know your:

- *password* to access the device or to clear your ID.
- *code name* (if your name is john, you could be [Juliet] or blue or any other name that your teammates can identify but cannot be ID by another group or state).
- call sign: your call sign might be related to your group if you are part of a unit. This could be "scout 1" (or scout 2 and scout 3), especially if you have 3 groups in the field.

a. Have enough batteries. Where possible don't use battery operated appliances in a long-term survival situation. If you are going to be in the bush for months then have re-chargeable batteries and a way to charge them if using such devices.

b. Check codes for your radios (this can be debilitating in a real situation), batteries, and check that all operators / students / survivalist have their frequency before setting off on your journey. Learn from the Desert Storm war where a small team of 8 SAS operators didn't have the correct codes and frequencies and could not call in an evacuation helicopter.

1. Even better than a radio is a **frequency scanner**, then you can listen to hundreds of different channels, and some can even change from UHF to VHF and FM. Get a robust

waterproof and reliable radio where financially viable as it will be used when no maintenance will be available, and it might be your only option for listening to any enemy transmissions.

a. Some frequency scanners might not have a talk facility.
b. Like all equipment you need to be able to recharge the unit with a solar charger or new batteries.
c. It should also be **robust** and *waterproof* for outdoor use.
d. This will also allow you to listen to military channels and medical services as well Ham radio channels.

Clothing

Camouflage clothing is discussed in length in the section on camouflaging.

Keep your civilian clothes in your bag while you use the camouflage, if it's a civil unrest situation where you do not want to be picked up, otherwise a **_low-key dress_** will be better in an urban environment. Don't wear bright colors that stick out unless you want to be seen, as in a rescue where the search party must locate you. Light non-descript clothes that have earthy colors are best for most situations and can blend in with most situations you will find yourself in. Wear your camouflage when it will come in useful when you are hunting or in an E&E as in a SHTF situation where being covert is best.

Warm clothing

You will need warm clothes; ***warm clothes are even used in the desert because it gets cold at night.*** You might find this hard to do with a 3-day bag so might need to consider thermal long johns and a reflective tarpaulin because the thermal long johns are light and can be compact in a compressed bag. Thermal reflective tarpaulin can be strong and light and can allow an increase in your nighttime heat retention and makes life easier even when having only a small fire.

Wet-weather clothing

Rain wear, rain jacket, poncho, plastic bag. A large army raincoat can suffice as a small expedient emergency shelter, so can a poncho, a plastic bag is a final effort to keep dry but can help in an emergency. The shelter sheet is a good all-round piece of kit that can help keep you dry and a little warmer than if you did not have it.

Socks and boots

Excellent quality **socks (wool) and boots** are probably the next most important things if not the most important because you need to walk everywhere, getting out of the situation as well as collecting food and water. ***Boots need to be worn in***, so don't just go and hike when you buy new boots, you will regret it. Leather is a very practical material for boots but is very heavy. Gortex material allows boots to breath and allows moisture out but does not allow rain in. The boot must be strong and allow your ankle protection, that's the whole idea behind having boots, it does also give limited protection against snake bites to the foot area, and the best for snake bite protection would be leather as it's tougher than most other light materials. Ideally you should have 2 pairs of boots that can be worn beforehand, so that you can stash one and wear one. ***This will be more for a long-term survival situation but can be applied to a SHTF situation*** where you might not be getting back to a town any time soon.

Bodywear

Pants and shirt: the clothing also depends on the environment you will be operating in e.g., a heavy material (tough) because a thick undergrowth with **thorns** will puncture thin material. ***Long pants*** and shirt will be more appropriate if you are in an ***African bush situation*** as long pants protect against scrub (harsh bush) and thorns. Shorts can be worn because of the heat as it gets extremely hot in the desert areas of Africa. Snakes and thorn trees are very numerous in the African bush. If you are not incredibly careful and aware of where you walk then wear leather boots and long pants, otherwise shorts and light boots might be sufficient. Whether you wear long pants and shirt or not in an African environment also depends on your **conditioning** to the ***climate and conditions.*** Most operators in the Rhodesian wars against communist insurgency wore short pants for tracking and counter insurgency operations. This was also used by the police on the SWA border because it's cooler and lighter. Bushmen don't wear any shoes, but ***their feet are conditioned to the environment.***

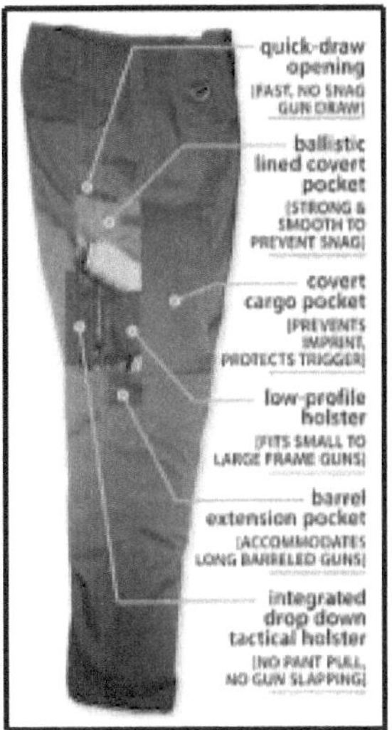
quick-draw
opening
(FAST, NO SNAG
GUN DRAW)

ballistic
lined covert
pocket
(STRONG &
SMOOTH TO
PREVENT SNAG)

covert
cargo pocket
(PREVENTS
IMPRINT,
PROTECTS TRIGGER)

low-profile
holster
(FITS SMALL TO
LARGE FRAME GUNS)

barrel
extension pocket
(ACCOMMODATES
LONG BARRELED GUNS)

integrated
drop down
tactical holster
(NO PANT PULL,
NO GUN SLAPPING)

Headwear

A hat is very practical in harsh environments where the sun will be beating down on you all day long, it **will protect your head** and serves to break up your outline if it's camouflage and used in a tactical environment. Use a hat that **allows air flow** and is light and **comfortable**, so you don't take it off. Camouflage caps can be **very warm** because of the material and scrim on it to help with camouflage, but that's the price you pay for camouflage. If you can, use a light comfortable camouflage cap. This will help especially in hunting to break your outline and yet won't make you hot. This is going to be the best for all round use, even in a SHTF context.

Hat with Mosquito net is shown below. This can be a good option all round as it protects the face from mosquitos and breaks up the outline a bit for a mild form of camouflage and the brim of the hat keeps it away from the face:

Mosquito Net

When you live in or are **going to an area with malaria, you will need a <u>mosquito net</u>** for evenings, this doesn't mean you have to have one, but to survive in comfort it does help. Keep in mind you can also use it to catch small fish and crabs in a river with this net, but *this might tear it*, forcing you to mend it in an emergency where you need it most for the mosquitos.

Electric Charger

Solar chargers are great if you have the equipment attachments to use them but make sure *they work with the type of equipment* you want to use them in. The flexible sheet types that you can get are quite durable and have a good power output.

a. Like with all equipment: test first
b. Must be **robust**
c. Light and compact
d. Give you the amount of power you need to power your equipment
e. *Light enough to carry.*

Rope/Cordage

This can be for anything that requires basic survival expertise. e.g., to tie down tarpaulins, shelter sheets, for making tarps, emergency climbing, and tie down your bundle before crossing a river. Paracord is a commonly used survival rope because it is light and strong. You can make cordage, but keep in mind if it's a prolonged SHTF situation you won't necessarily be able to or have time to make cordage or have the skill as there is limited time.

a. It should be strong and capable of being used in an emergency climbing situation if doubled and this will normally give you 25 meters of climbing capacity for a 50-meter rope. Only use nonclimbing rope for climbing when there is no other option, and you won't "make it out" (survive) if you don't i.e., emergency context.

b. Carry enough of the rope for your operation/survival. It's used for shelters, climbing trees, securing equipment, climbing cliffs, pulling vehicles out of trouble, moving large logs, traps for hunting, string for bows, string for bow drill etc.

c. Have the rope accessible but make sure it doesn't fall off and you lose it, usually put it at the top of your pack. When placed on the outside of the pack it tends to get hooked on bushes and shrubs and can give your position away so don't use this in a SHTF type scenario, rather put it on the inside at the top of the pack.

d. Know the *basic knots*, the very basics are needed to get by, but specialty knots can be useful, especially quick loosening knots and very secure knots when you don't want to lose a piece of equipment or want to abseil from a ridge to the bottom of a mountain.

e. Protect the rope from wear and tear, if possible, by using cloth to prevent it being damaged or frayed. Pack it correctly so that it's possible to be used and kept out of the way

f. Pack it away neatly so you can use it quickly when needed, rolling it up and keeping it neat is better than bundling it up all knotted up and then having to untie it.

Bankline (left) and paracord (right):

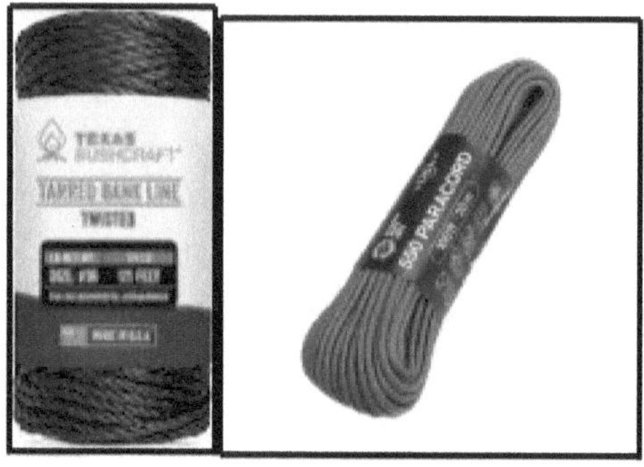

Binoculars

These should be **high quality, lightweight** and **_robust_** but go for quality and get one as **small as possible.** Binoculars allow you to search for game with more precision over long distances without getting too close, to assess what your plan of action will be to catch the game. You can also assess the layout of the land to look for a good camping/shelter place. It can also be used when tracking to look ahead for game that might be close enough to see with binoculars but not with the eye. Game such as warthogs is close to the ground and you might not see them from 500 meters away with your naked eye, spotting them will make it possible to stalk closer. An 8x20 or 10x20 is normally small and compact but light. The monocular is even better because of its small size and you can get superior quality and robust construction.

- a. Nikon
- b. Bushnell
- c. Steiner
- d. Docter

Monocular

The Docter monocular made in Germany has small, light and excellent glass. This would be an excellent monocular for reconnaissance.

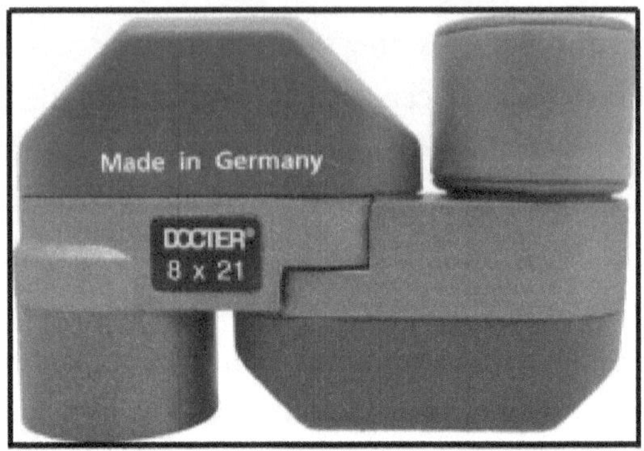

Night Vision

This is a specialized piece of equipment that costs more than most items such as binoculars, but these are good for searching your area, while in OP/LP, or searching for game at night (good moonlight) or low light situations. Also used for night walking and night driving but don't use it continuously because they can tire your eyes out. If possible, use your NV monocular for a fleeting period at a time to avoid fatigue and to have night vision in one eye at least. In some cases, you can even use a normal (non-NV) monocular in bright moonlight.

Night vision scope:

Thermal Imaging

Thermal imaging devices can help with spotting game and enemy at night with limited view through foliage, this can also assist with hunting. These come in small sizes, but you should assess what the benefits are for your situation because of the extra weight and space it will take up. It is ideal if you have space in your large bag which is for long-term survival purposes. Remember to obtain one that uses batteries or a charger that **can be charged with your solar charger**.

Sleeping Bag

The best combination for sleeping equipment is:

1. *Sleeping bag*: the temperature rating you want to use will depend on where you are and how long you will be in the area. You can go without sleep for a day or two but it's not good for prolonged periods. The warmer the sleeping bag normally the larger it is so if space is at a minimum, and then you might have to get a smaller sleeping bag and use layers to create heat i.e., layers of tarpaulin and *reflective materials* overhead and a *Gore-Tex Bivy* bag to do the rest.
2. *Inner liner of cotton* that can be washed. Cotton or silk that adds 3-5 degrees of temperature to your sleeping bag, this also keeps *inside cleaner*, allows you to *adjust warmth* to your situation which gives you *some flexibility.*
3. *Bivy bag: weatherproofs your sleeping bag* and keeps you warmer than if you only had the sleeping bag.

Dutch Gore-Tex Bivy (excellent sleeping equipment choice):

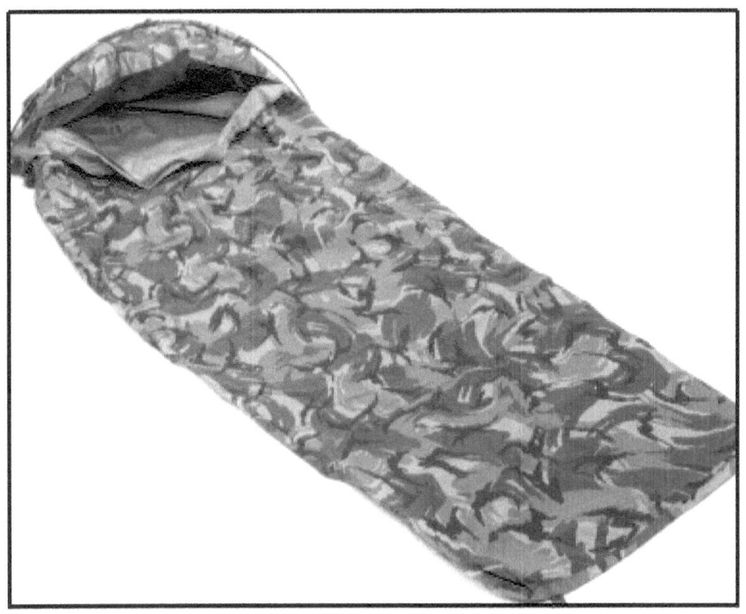

Large Plastic Bag

Use as weather protection or emergency sleeping bag or to put your whole backpack in it when in an emergency if you need to cache it. You can buy these at outdoor stores and are made specifically for survival.

Shelter Sheet

This is the easiest piece of equipment to make a quick expedient shelter with and this can be laid over the ground just to cover you or as a ground sheet to keep moisture away that emanates from the ground.

Carrying Your Equipment

If you are considering survival for a few months, you will at the very least need a large backpack (Fig 2b) with food (**this <u>won't carry all your food</u> as you will still need to catch and hunt**). If you want to be really prepared include a small bag, with other hard to make items for survival such as saws, blades (large and small blade for different chores), wire for traps, rope (paracord / bankline), compass, cooking pot, sleeping bags etc. The smaller **3-day** (see fig 1a) bags are only for *getting you to your designated area within 3 days*, which could be a nearby farm or a village, where you can apply long term survival techniques and tactics.

The 3-day bag isn't designed for long term survival itself; otherwise, it would be **called a 30-day bag or something like that**. Unless you are a Bushman, and you happen to get stranded in the Kalahari Desert, because then a small bag would be good for months. This is because **their knowledge is extensive,** and they can live off the land for months. Knowing what is edible and where to find food and water is essential especially in environments such as arid grassland or deserts.

Bushmen can travel very light as they are experts at survival:

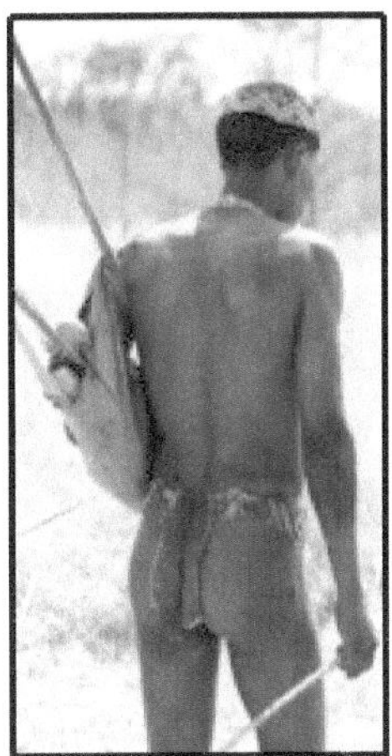

You can also **have a few different types of bags** (Backpack) and **different size bags** dedicated to different items. These *backpacks you will have to put in whatever transport you use*, this could be a vehicle /plane or boat etc. then when you get to the area you will operate in, you can carry the **smaller bags dedicated to specific items such as saw, axe and fire making** and then placed in an individual cache site your larger less used items. Mark the site on your map and make mental notes of landmarks in case you lose your map (not if it's a *military type of operation then your route and caches are secret*).

What you carry and how you carry the equipment also depends on the tactical (a combat **situation** or non-permissive situation) situation what is happening on the ground, for example has the natural disaster caused a bit of civil unrest scenario or even a war? War or SHTF type situations will mean carrying weapons as well as being concerned by survival and hunting fishing or foraging for wild edibles.

Backpack Selection Guide

Keep in mind that the situation, scenario, you are training and purpose of your outing **will primarily dictate** the type and **size of backpack** you will use. For hunting you could use a plain 50lt (liter) bag. One main pocket (packing area) as you will not need to access your night vision optical device quickly or your spare ammunition or magazines. Your training and experience will dictate what you carry in your bag.

When making a list for your specific backpack in *your context*, **conditions (war/ SHTF /civil unrest /general survival), environment,** and **weather,** you must *pack accordingly*. This means in a *hot environment* you only need a *basic sleep system*, which means less cover is needed. In a cold environment you need an extensive sleep system with protection below your inflatable mattress, a very warm sleep system, and overhead protection with reflective material above you. *All these aspects should be applied when planning your equipment list.* In cold environments you will also need more food as your metabolism will be burning lots of food, your movement and stress will cause you to burn more than normal (*high energy environment*).

Backpack/Bergen

Choose a 50-100 liter *depending on operational needs*. It *must fit properly* and must not cause unneeded stress or strain that can be debilitating for a person in an *already* stressful situation. Do not hang carabiners on the outside, don't hang bottles and other things which imbalance you. These things will also tend to hook on things. Put everything in the backpack as much as possible. Items you can put on the outside are things like your last-ditch survival bag. Which is a small pouch with survival items. That is if you don't have a belt webbing kit.

1. For 3-day patrolling or reconnaissance you might only need 30 to 50-liter bag and chest webbing which might weigh 10-20 kg *depending on what your SOPs* (standard operating procedures) are. The reason for patrolling will decide what weight you carry – combat patrol will be heavier with ammunition. You might have a contact loadout and an E&E loadout when on ambush patrol. Contact loadout might be 3-6 magazines in a pouch in front of you for initial contact in an ambush then once empty move out and break contact with the enemy.

2. Doing a 2–3-week patrol and recon you might need an 80 to 100-liter bag **depending on your resupply situation**, which may mean you have to take all the gear e.g., SA SF need 2-3 weeks operating equipment as there will be no resupply possible.

3. Main pack with sleeping bag, food, extra clothes (socks/underclothes), NV/Thermal, batteries, water etc. For some situations you might carry extra ammunition for prolonged patrolling and combat. This would be high and close to your back in backpack for balance and ease of

access.

4. Depending on your function, there is an extra combat load for ambush patrols as once you ***shoot most of your ammunition out in a contact***, you will still ***need ammo to get home***, which is the reason for an ***extra bag with contact ammo*** and ammo in your belt webbing.

5. Make sure you have some way of ***waterproofing your bag*** as this will be important if you cross a river. Options include:

    a. Spray with water proofing spray

    b. Use heavy duty trash bags inside for contents of bag

    c. Rain cover over the whole bag designed to keep backpack dry

    d. Use ***purpose built dry bag*** on inside for contents or extra emergency water supply

Purpose built dry bags: this is an essential survival item especially for combat survival as a protector of sensitive equipment and emergency water reservoir and so on.

Small 'Day Bag'

A small day bag would normally suffice for a 2 to 5-day hike out of a survival situation; a larger bag means you can have a slight bit more than just the basics and is obviously a better option but not absolutely needed. You can improvise a blanket bag or even make a basket from small flexible branches; this will of course be only in a long-term survival situation.

Small day bag:

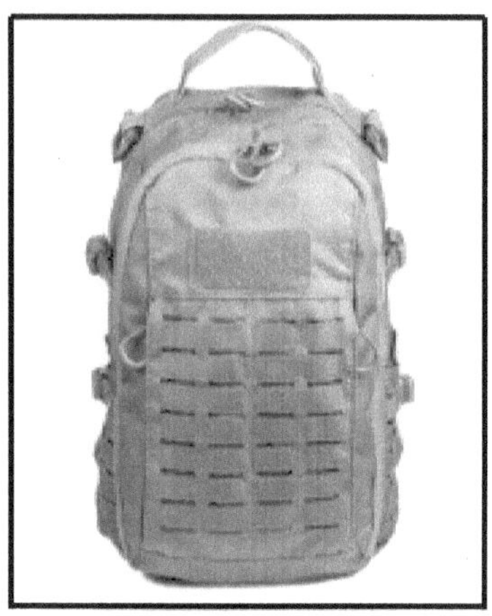

Basic Backpack

Backpack: 3-5day bag is about 15-20 liters or a large one 40-to-50-liter bag (you can use this or bigger depending on the type of situation you wish to prepare for). ***3-day bags are light and easy to walk with*** and have enough space for a few days' food – this doesn't have to be more than 5-10kg. This can also have a folding saw, large or small blade or both, water, binoculars, fire making equipment and a shelter sheet that can be light and compact. This should suffice for e.g., a hunting trip as you do not normally move far from a hunting lodge and will be accompanied by a hunting guide. On hunting when walking you will only need a small bag with the basics to keep on you.

Bags could potentially be as such, a 60 liter or slightly smaller.

Large Backpack

Large packs are going to be much heavier and could weigh 20 to 50 kg loadout when full, depending on what you want to put into it. Are your ***objectives*** for survival or hunting? Large packs are used when you will be in the field for ***2 to 4 weeks***.

The standard SA infantry bag makes a good medium sized bag for medium to long term use; it is a good color and has enough space for more than just 3 days.

For civil unrest or SHTF, a good bag for long term survival will be about 80–100-liters. Large bags are **not for a fast-moving combat** situation because of the weight, they are for situations where you need to ***hold up in a place for a few weeks*** and need to carry in enough to **sustain you till you can get to know the ground.** Knowing the foods in the area, game types and trails that lead to water and how to catch/hunt the game in your AO (area of operations). Natural food sources are not always as appetizing as crops grown on a farm. Long term planning means seeds and fruit trees, though this will need to be on a ***plot owned by you*** and not close to any well-used roads or large settlements (where it could be raided).

Consider 85-liter capacity backpack for longer duration than 5 days. You can realistically carry 2-3 weeks supply food in a bag like this but not enough water as well, as you might need 2-3 liters for heavy workload and extreme conditions. The water load alone will come to 63 liters i.e., 63 kg. This load will work out to over 100kg just for food and water, and ***that's not practical for patrolling and operating***. Therefore, a water source is the only practical option for longer term operations. A practical load would be 3-5 days water and 2-3 weeks food with other combat essentials and then procure water when in your AO (area of operations).

80-liter pack left and 50-liter pack right:

Large backpack for extended patrolling/reconnaissance or long-term survival:

A heavy-duty backpack for hunting and survival or SHTF can be useful but keep in mind the ***weight can be debilitating*** if you are not trained for the type of weight and can cause an injury, so it's suggested you only attempt this with proper training.

This is a heavy-duty bag for serious hunting and survival, you can see the bottom in the first picture has metal frames a metal carrier, ledge, or shelf. A metal frame is stronger than the plastic frames, and technically should allow you to carry more weight than a normal frameless bag which tends to feel heavier than normal.

Waterproof Backpack

This would be a good idea for Jungle travel and survival. It's a totally waterproof backpack so that all your items remain dry it can and should be used to cross the multiple waterways/rivers you find in the jungle. For the most sensitive items and for water carrying capacity have a dry bag inside as well.

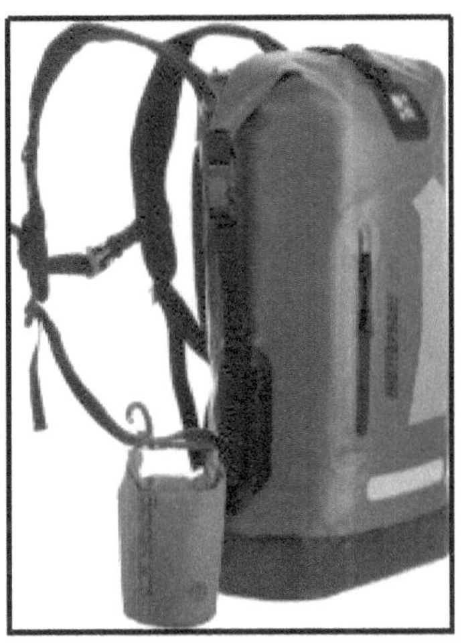

Packing Your Backpack

Backpacks with compartments on the *outside* allow you to pack stuff like cooking and medical equipment on the outside *for quick access*. Other items that can be placed on the outside pockets are quick energy foods, water and **water purifying equipment**, chemicals for purifying, **ammunition** and binoculars/ NV/thermal should also be quickly accessible (if *traveling*, hunting at night). You can also pack rain gear on the outside if space allows. Your clothes are packed inside *water resistant bags* (dry bag). It is not just your clothes that need to be protected from water, this applies to your electronic equipment as well as food (it will spoil), weapons and auxiliary equipment e.g. firearm magazines, and other delicate equipment that needs to be kept dry such as books etc.

The backpack is packed with **lighter** stuff **below** and **heavier** to the **middle upper** part of the pack *closer to your body* as a rule. The reason for the *heavy stuff* going in middle is because if it were too **high** up then it would pull you over and **imbalance you**. If it is too low, it's more uncomfortable to carry. If it is in the middle or slightly higher than the middle, then it is easier to carry and not going to imbalance you. Also keep in mind you want equipment that you use on a continuous basis to be packed near the top of the opening of the bag. This is for balance and efficiency.

Sleeping bags and tarpaulin can be packed on the outside at top but it must be **waterproofed**. If the sleeping bag is on top then ensure its waterproof otherwise you might find yourself with a wet bag. You need to **_sleep well_** to **recover quickly** and fully. This can be achieved by having a backpack cover that is camouflaged and waterproof. This is even made better and more efficient when you also have a layer which is **reflective below** the tarpaulin or shelter sheet facing down in cold and facing up or away from you in the heat (sun). The shelter sheet should be water resistant and preferably camouflaged. ***It is always better to be low profile*** than to be easily detected, as in civil unrest SHTF or war you want to be low profile.

Try to keep the camouflage as close to the terrain coloration as possible. See below where the camouflage is for a dry terrain: It means both large patterns and micro patterns with correct colors.

Same covering layer from a distance:

Belt Webbing context

Another option is to have a **belt webbing** that goes with your pack that allows you to **drop your main pack** and move on with the belt webbing, till you can come back to your main backpack. This might be to recon an area, or as **response to contact** with the enemy, for hunting game getting water, setting traps, or looking for food, looking for a weapon such as spear to hunt boar or small game, looking for signs of water. You must know exactly **where you put** the pack and how to **get back to it**. A quick solution if you do not have time to bury it is to suspend it in a tree using your parachute cord (paracord). *The belt webbing only carries basic survival equipment* and isn't meant for long term survival **but** if packed properly and correctly used, it can be effective for survival over an extended period. The amount of time you can survive with your belt webbing is determined by your level of **training** (Tracking, finding wild edibles), **experience** (how much time you spent in bush) and **expertise** (knowledge of how to trap game, make fire etc.).

Example of belt webbing (UK Army) on the left and SA SF belt webbing on the right:

Bushmen use extraordinarily little equipment when they travel but they can survive indefinably in the bush because they have <u>very good bush knowledge</u>.

This should be your goal to be like the bushman in self-sufficiency. They drink very little water live in one of the hottest environments known to man and very little equipment. Their equipment might sometimes only consist of a knife, small bow ostrich egg for water and fire making equipment. That doesn't weigh more than 2-3 kg total.

What you carry your survival equipment in e.g., the type of bag/belt webbing/vest and what you carry in that container (webbing) is dictated by what you need it for. In other words, are you going into the wilds to hunt or watch birds, walking trip or are you just carrying it for a potential survival situation while in the bush? As a game ranger it's part of your job to walk around in nature as in the areas as a game guard, game guide, nature enthusiast etc.

Belt webbing was initially used for military purposes but can also be used for carrying your **basic survival equipment** for outdoor hiking and camping. **Small vests are sometimes used for <u>reconnaissance</u>** purposes and larger vests are used as a survival and weight bearing vest for gear and ammo. Chest webbing is used for carrying ammo, so we won't be discussing these in this section of the training. **The belt webbing** must be **comfortable and able to easily carry the weight** you put in. This could be 5 to 10 kg depending on the situation you are preparing for. It's only for carrying **basic** equipment in a survival situation and the basic combat load in a SHTF. Basics of survival water (water purifying), fire, one small shelter sheet, compass, blade, monocular. You then have extra magazines for combat if this is applicable to your scenario.

Belt webbing general considerations

The *belt webbing* should be your **last line of survival equipment** and should have *basic needs for survival* such as fire making, water bottle and canteen to boil water, monocular, very basic shelter sheet. This can also include spare socks and underclothes.

1. Basic survival equipment, fire, water, coms (communication), 1-2 days food (this is dependent on what your energy expenditure is and genetic predisposition), knife for processing game/wood fighting, **compass/GPS** (location), night vision (small evening mobility device), water bottle with canteen cup to boil water, water purifying tabs, **water filter** etc.

2. Optional or additional to chest webbing can be 4 magazines in your belt webbing of 30 rounds for a total of 120 rounds should be your **E&E loadout**. This brings the total load of ammunition in chest webbing and belt webbing to **300 rounds**. An E&E load means the last-ditch running loadout that allows you to *break contact* and *move away* from the contact with enough essential items of survival, which is your belt webbing loadout.

3. As a side note, **when storing your magazines** make sure they are well oiled, but **when using** them then *remove the oil especially in a desert /sandy environment* as the sand will stick to the **oil and cause a stoppage**. The only **exception to this rule is when at sea** then you might consider oiling the spring and on the inside of the magazine to stop it from rusting and then wash them with hot water and soap when back at your base camp, then re oil if you are at the coast. That is if you happened to go out to sea.

Belt Webbing essential items and comprehensive list

Only carry the very essential items, in your belt webbing. Consider the items in the list below might not all fit into your belt kit so *consider your objectives and <u>operational</u> requirements*

The items you carry in your belt kit will be dictated by the terrain (weather), context (simple survival or combat survival), hunting, or fishing and so on. The basics stay the same, keep it simple and don't carry anything unnecessary. Keep in mind the Bushmen carry very little. Westerners tend to carry way more than they need to when hunting.

1. Fire making: 3 or 4 ways (methods) to make fire, that you know are dependable and you are very familiar with. Having 2 very reliable means can also be doable if you combine this with the fact that you can also make a friction fire if you have the skills to do so.

2. Water carrying and purification (a straw that filters water allows you to drink straight out of the stream /lake /river and is most convenient for combat survival)

3. Medical small bag with **basics**: (basic for trauma). These are basic items, but the understanding is not that basic, so learning how to use these items is slightly more complicated and must be mastered to know how to apply them in correct context e.g., if you get shot, as seconds count in a major bleed made by for instance a femoral artery wound.

   a. Tourniquet (heavy bleeding from a limb), not to be applied to the neck!
   b. blood clotting agent

c. trauma bandage (to help absorb blood and close area off to hemorrhaging)

d. you can also consider suture, antiseptic cream, triple antibiotic cream

e. butterfly plasters and other small items for closing minor cuts

f. Basic all-around pain killer such as Myprodol (generic is Mybulen), use the kind that affect your joints the least.

1. Small amount of energy food source, high energy food peanuts and raisins, corn syrup (this is not good long term or if you have insulin sensitivity). Honey is a high energy food and can be put on cuts as a wound healing. Dried fruit, oats (long term energy) slow release and maybe even rice – brown rice doesn't last as long as white rice but brown rice is better for you.

a. Making homemade energy bars fresh and then vacuum packing them is a great way to ensure you get the most out of what you carry for food.

b. Combination of 800 grams peanut butter plus 700 grams Nutella with 1kg oats will give you combined calories of 35 000 calories (translates to 11 meals worth of energy. It should not be for normal use as this might give <u>you **low blood sugar**</u> due to the high sugar in the Nutella). Peanut butter has a lot of **oil and protein**, and oats is long term energy. This is not healthy, but it will suffice in a combat and survival situation for a short period of time where oil, protein, and sugar are needed for quick energy and carbohydrates. Keep in mind low carbs with high vegetables (when at home) and meats with fats are proven to be best for performance and endurance. Meats and fats give you the best satisfying hunger which means you stay feeling 'full' for longer and thus less hungry.

c. This high energy peanut butter and Nutella will be ok for *high energy expenditure* like survival and **high intensity activities**. Especially where you are walking the whole day as your body will burn all the energy you take in virtually immediately. Don't use this combination if you will be in a sedentary situation like a hide doing reconnaissance as the high energy for the sugar in the Nutella will make you **tense and fidgety**. *Then use slow burning energies* like fats, oats, proteins, vegetables etc. Sugary foods might be better for hard walking and climbing mountains.

d. *Any sugary supplement can make you very hungry* (due to insulin given off mopping up blood sugar) so consider your state of health and your ability to deal with sugar. From the age of 40 on your body will deal less efficiently with sugar so then rather choose long slow energy foods like oats, nuts, oils such as coconut, dried fruit, and biltong (dried meat).

e. Protein in either dried meat (biltong) or pemmican is also an excellent meat source and can last for years. Drying meat in the sun or with salt as a preservative will both dry the meat and keep it stable and good.

1. Binoculars/monocular

a. You can use a monocular if you don't have a greater than 6x magnification or 10x magnification scope on your rifle, but a scope with 6x magnification is more than enough for hunting and surveillance. Shoot small game with 22LR and larger game with 308 or similar caliber.

b. It does help to have a monocular to check a game animal or to check ahead during reconnaissance, as it is light and can be stowed in a pocket for quick access. A monocular is *lighter and takes up less space* and you can get very high magnification. 8-10x magnification can be enough.

1. Radio or **frequency scanner** combination hand-held two-way radio. The frequency scanner allows you to listen to aircraft, police radio and other emergency services as well as many other radio signals.

a. Frequency scanners are great for understanding the situation that you are in.
b. The information can help you to determine your next move to make as you travel or hold up in a camp.
c. Two-way radios give you the ability to coordinate with fellow survivalists or operators. This will be of great value in a SHTF situation. This is because reporting enemy activity is very important for a small group of survivalists.
d. Communications will also be important for reporting your location if you are looking for game or reporting a medical situation.

1. Compass: standard prismatic /GPS/watch compass or
button compass for back up and map. Having 2-3 means of

direction finding is beneficial but not absolute as *learning the lay of the land is best.*

a. This would be very important in a SHTF situation as heading to a point in an operation is very important and needs to be accurate and timely.

b. Losing your way is not beneficial to you in a survival situation, **this is inefficient** and can cause more stress on your organization as you stay in field without achieving your goal.

c. *Knowing the general lay of the land* is important so that you cannot get lost. Once you know where the *prominent mountain ranges* are, and general large land features, will make it easier to navigate the landscape.

d. Following rivers and mountain ranges, if possible, can also be a handy way of navigating (called "handrailing").

1. Good quality full tang fixed blade and small folding blade for the pocket. Large blades are for heavy duty work and the small knife (multipurpose tool) one to make small traps, cutting string and other small tasks.

2. Small LED light (preferably recharged with solar), this is light and small and is only used for small tasks around the camp or for surreptitiously reading a map at night and as an emergency light. It's also as an emergency light if you drop something at night and this is why I keep mine on the outside of the pack easily accessible.

3. Some paracord or bankline (tar covered rope) for making guidelines for tent /shelter, making traps, making a pack from wood and string, or rope for climbing in an emergency, as proper climbing rope is thick and cumbersome to allow for a lot of strength and stretch.

4. Bivy bag and or ground sheet. Both would be good as you

sleep on the one and in the Bivy bag. Having an overhead shelter would be even better; this should be a reflective layer and a camouflage layer which will be the outer layer.

5. Shelter sheet that can be used as covering overhead:

a. Quick shelter for shade and protection from rain
b. Cover is better if in a camouflaged pattern
c. Cover when hunting to hide from game
d. Covering when in hot terrain with additional reflective sheet in addition to the covering sheet (Bivy sheet/tarp)

Example of tarp use:

1. A small **compact NV device** will come in very handy (it must be very robust and remember the batteries or solar charger to recharge).

a. This can be used for reconnaissance
b. Game viewing, hunting
c. It will also become very useful in a SHTF scenario
d. It will be very important in E&E situation as escaping and evading means knowing where the enemy is without them

seeing you.

1. A small robust thermal imager would even be better for nighttime hunting but remember the **batteries will need to be carried for long term use**. The technology is at a point where you can carry a very small light thermal image that is as small as a box of twenty cigarettes. The benefit is massive so carrying one should be a prerequisite for any type of SHTF scenario.

a. This can be used for reconnaissance when used to scan an area for enemy presence when doing a close area reconnaissance as you might not need magnification when close enough – you just need to know if the enemy are close.
b. It can be used for game viewing, hunting and reconnaissance when doing military operations or in a hunting party. From a point of hunting the game can be seen without them knowing. This is a huge advantage in reality.
c. It will also become extremely useful in a SHTF scenario when scanning terrain from an OP (observation post) / LP (listening post).
d. It will be very important in E&E situation as escaping and evading means knowing where the enemy is without them seeing you.

Thermal imager:

1. Survival items in a tin or plastic container (doubles as food container when needed): fishing line, hooks sinker, scalpel, steel or copper wire for snare, commando saw, button compass, suture, small magnifying glass, fire steel, pain killers, medication for diarrhea. Any item you feel you will need where you are in that specific type of environment.
2. Small solar panel can be useful for any long-term survival scenario

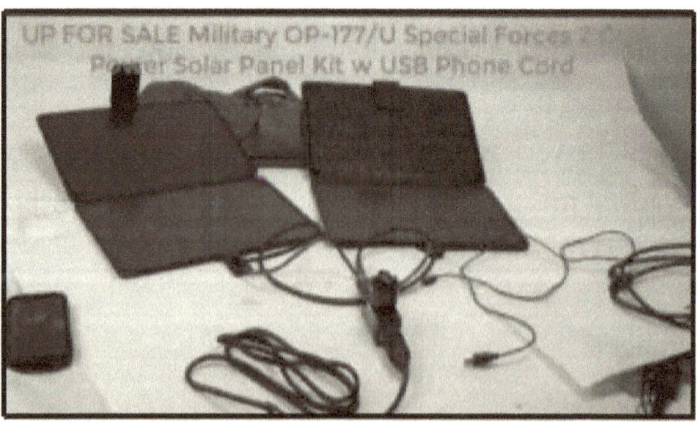

Button compass: Example of a survival tin and contents:

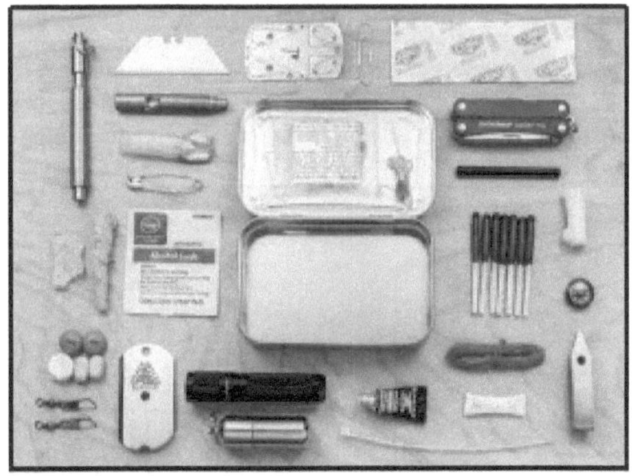

Think for yourself as this is what you will need to do in the field so start now and learn to trust your own abilities and **instincts** and be flexible in training so you can be flexible in your actual survival situation.

A 3-day bag in desert tan:

See section on survival bags

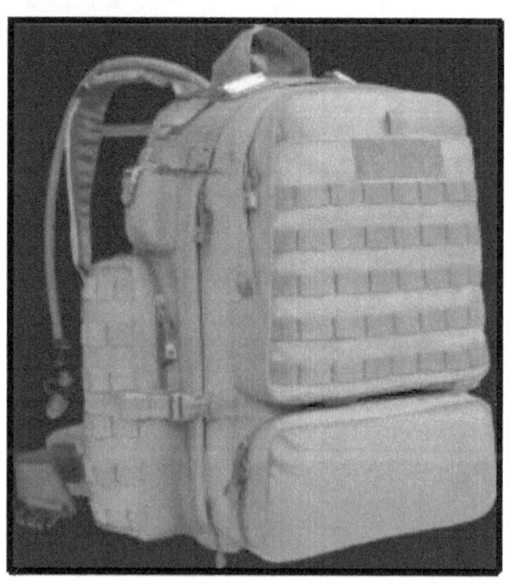

Assault webbing without disruptive pattern painted on (SA infantry/Parra bats):

The first picture shows the belt webbing on the operator and the second picture what it looks like close up:

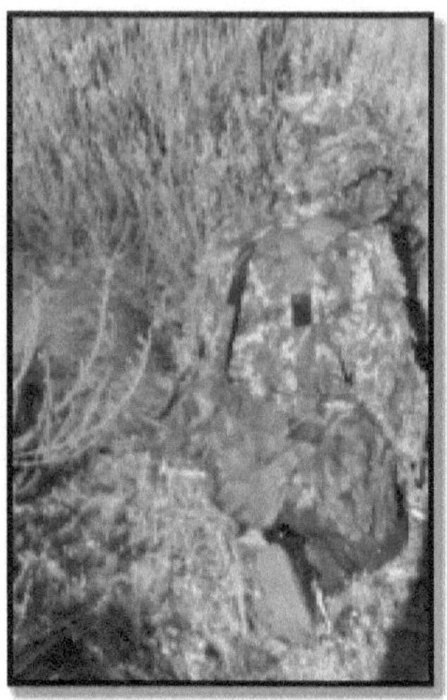

Belt webbing close up with blended colors, all the basic essentials of survival are found in this bag (carrier): This was camouflaged for reconnaissance

Light Vest/Assault Webbing

You might also consider a *lighter load bearing vest*, sometimes **called assault webbing,** this is similar in function to the British belt webbing, and allows or forces (due to limited space) you to *carry lighter* when in your operational area while your ***main supply is cached*** somewhere safe and easy to find and accessible. The lighter assault webbing also allows you to carry ammunition conveniently that is accessible while having fire making equipment and other essential survival items at hand, such as drinking straw for drinking from contaminated water sources. This is the advantage of *combat type webbing that doubles as survival gear*. You might be in a SHTF type scenario but also need to hunt and trap for food. This webbing will then double as a survival vest and a combat webbing if the situation demands it.

Pictured below is assault webbing used by SASF during 80-90s with added colors for increased effectiveness and large pattern discernment as discussed in the camouflage manual that I wrote and is available for purchase:

One carry option, if the combat situation allows, is to drape your assault webbing over your main bag, then **cache the main bag** at the appropriate place (destination AO = area of operations) and continue with you assault webbing. This is so you can **carry light for reconnaissance with minimum gear** and patrolling the area (looking for water, shelter, food, and fire making essentials depending on your situation) carrying most of the heavy stuff in the main bag. This is the same use that is applied to belt webbing where the main load is carried in main bag and belt webbing is for essential equipment and survival gear.

Pouch Or Tin for survival items

Some people carry very little for **survival such as a tin** with basic survival items in that they can carry on them all the time also called (EDC or everyday carry). In the case of an emergency this only contains the very minimum equipment. Things such as fire starters (matches/fire steel/ flint and steel) water purifying tablets, scalpel, wire for traps, plasters, small multi-purpose knife, small candles, tin foil and maybe some tinder (tinder in case there is nothing to start your fire with). Other options if space in the tin is available could be small quality button compass, wire saw (these are normally very flimsy and break easily)

Equipment for SHTF or Combat

SHTF or Combat loadout will be dictated by *what the enemy carries and* how volatile the situation is, which means considering if you are expecting *large groups of combatants* or *just an odd criminal* in a SHTF type scenario. It will mean the following elements will play a role; combat will require *high-capacity magazines*. For survival you will therefore need a blade, and basic cover shelter sheet, and pistol for self-defense will do. Your 308 or 223 Cal *semi auto rifle* will be your *hunting and fighting weapon*. You will most probably have a large well-equipped backpack/Bergen. This will be cached while doing any reconnaissance / hunting / foraging. This means that a large *backpack will hold survival items* and your *webbing will contain your combat equipment* as well as *some survival items*.

Full SHTF webbing layout

Say you have a backpack, chest webbing and belt webbing. These weights are based on my loadout, which weighs about 25-30kg:

1. The main *comfort items* will be in the backpack, this could weigh 15-20 kg or more depending on *operational requirements*.
2. The *combat load* in the *chest webbing*, this could weigh 2-8kg, depending on the amount of firearm magazines.
3. The *survival items* and some aspects of combat load in *belt webbing*. This could weigh about 5-8kg.

This will *spread the load and weight of all the items evenly*. This can still be heavy, and you should *choose very carefully*. Extra weight will be very heavy if you have to walk to an RV (rendezvous) point 20-30 km away then still make shelter, recon the area, and stand guard. Cut away any unwanted webbing straps and don't carry 3 or 4 items of fire making equipment or any other unnecessary items. If you only carry 2 fire items make sure you tie it to your pants belt so you don't lose it.

Shown below is an example loadout. You will notice there is not a lot of "scrims" (grass colored material) just a small amount hanging off the sleeves, as you do not need a lot to break your outline.

We now cover these loadout aspects in more detail:

Chest webbing

1. Carry a combat load of say 6-mags of 30 rounds each, thus 180 rounds of 223/5.56x45 caliber ammo, this can also be for reconnaissance if needed even though ***you do want to carry very light*** for reconnaissance. As an example, a reconnaissance operator in South African SF told me he carried 3 AK magazines on a recon mission because the total weight of operational gear could be anything from 80-100 Kg for a small team SF operation. Keep in mind SA SF do not have the extraction and resupply resources that other militaries have when operational behind enemy lines.

2. If the chest webbing is your only carrying means, then you might consider a compass, and radio for situations where you might be in a team type SHTF situation. This does not mean you don't have anything on your belt as ***you could have a small survival pouch and belt knife with water bottle and canteen cup***. This does not constitute belt webbing but can get you by on a short duration mission.

3. This is also assuming you have a knife on your belt as well as a water bottle on the belt as standard carry if you know how to set up your belt webbing. Some like to carry a basic trauma kit for bullet or puncture wounds. Things such as ***hemostatic gauze*** or quick clot and ***pressure bandage*** with ***tourniquet.*** These suffice for a basic combat operation.

4. Standard EDC (everyday carry) should also consist of a multipurpose knife (e.g., Leatherman brand), lighter and ferro rod in your pockets ***at minimum.*** You could also fit a compass and magnifying glass (with a small packet of tinder) in your pocket.

5. This will make your chest webbing into a ***first line of survival***, if set up correctly, which will allow you to have a

basic line of **defense (survival)** in a survival situation as well as make fire to boil water or cook and make very basic shelter. For emergencies that is good enough.

6. If you had all these pieces of *survival items* or equipment in your ***belt webbing***, then you might choose to omit some items from your chest webbing, this is because having the same items in your chest webbing and belt will be excessive weight and inefficient.

7. This means you do not need chest webbing if you have survival equipment ***and belt webbing*** although you do want to have at least fire-starting equipment in both belt and chest webbing as this is very light and small and reasonable to carry.

Caching extra supplies

Remember **you can bury** (cache) some of the stuff at a point where you and your teammates can access them later. It must be properly sealed before caching (burying) as the ground tends to breakdown or rust certain types of containers. Water and moisture seem to get into the best sealed containers so make sure it is well sealed, if this is what you plan to do. Make sure the site of the cache is <u>**very clearly marked**</u> (**marked for <u>you</u>** not so anybody else can access your equipment) and that you can find your way back to this point easily enough day or night. When placing your cache have 2 or 3 ways of recognizing the place of the cache. This is because one can be moved or taken away by weather or man. Always keep in mind *safety issues* when approaching your cache as its virtually impossible to obliterate all sigh of your passing and cache site.

Later in this manual we'll look at caches in more detail.

Survival Kits

Example of Essential Survival Bag and Items

Survival bag with essentials for survival:

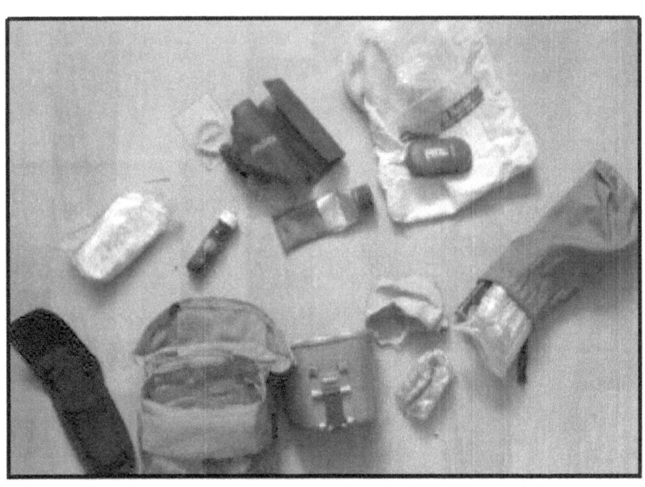

More specific on contents of the survival bag
Metal cup Headlamp (see picture above for size context)

Fire lighters (left) and Esbit stove and lighter (right)

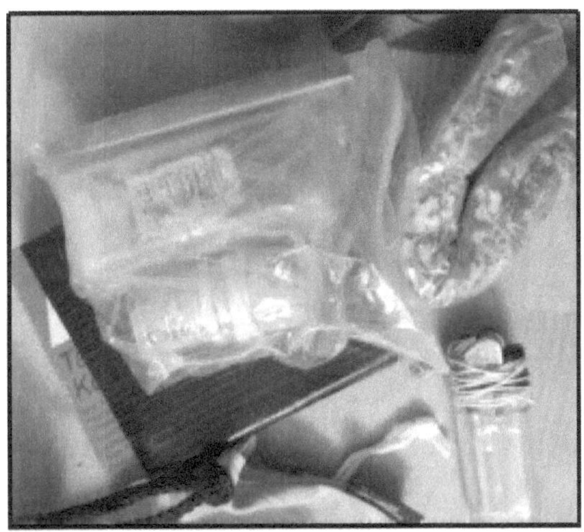

Multitool Potassium permanganate Compass

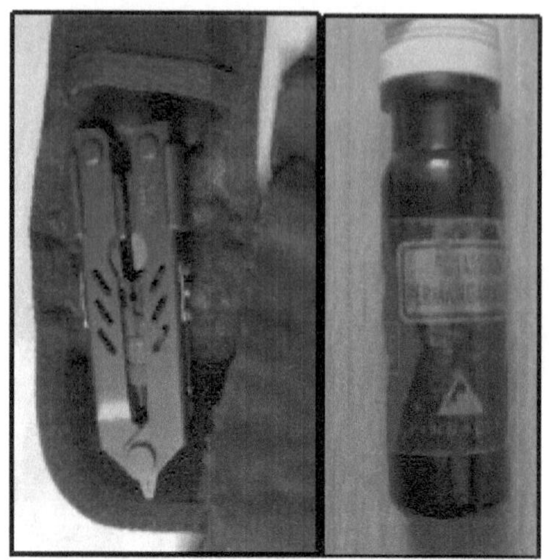

Large Survival Kit Items

These can be placed in a larger tin or utility pouch, waterproof (Samsonite small container).

Consider the following categories:

1. Fire

   a. Fire steel (on your belt or in your pocket)
   b. Magnifying glass (this can be placed back-to-back with signal mirror)
   c. 5-10 matches waterproof if possible
   d. Lighter
   e. Cotton wool is used to hold items and for tinder

1. Water

   a. Condom for carrying one liter
   b. Purification tabs
   c. Water purifying straw
   d. Fire will purify water
   e. 3-liter water bag (fill when needed)

1. Food

   a. Stainless/titanium cup/ fire bucket
   b. Snare wire
   c. Hooks and nylon (also a sinker and float)
   d. Small Net (multipurpose cover head against mosquito /catch fish etc.)

1. Shelter

a. Plastic bag (space blanket)
b. Reflective blanket one side reflective other side olive green (permanent one, not the temporary one)
c. Commando saw
d. Small multipurpose knife/tool
e. 2-3 meters duct tape (tape around camouflage cream or similar)

1. Camouflage

a. Camouflage cream (minimum small two-tone green and sand)
b. Mud and natural vegetation can be used (vegetation cut with commando saw)

1. Medical

a. Anti-septic cream (triple antibiotic cream)
b. Diarrhea meds
c. Tweezers
d. Magnifying glass listed above is used for **fire** and to **take out splinters**
e. Scalpel
f. 5-10 plasters (Butterfly plasters, large and small ones)
g. Tourniquet (handmade or bought)
h. Blood clotting agent e.g., Celox
i. Salt for dehydration

1. Direction finding

a. Button compass or larger compass
b. Your watch can be a pro-trek or something like that that gives you another back up direction idea

c. GPS if your bag is big enough

1. Signaling

a. Signal mirror
b. Fire is also used for signal
c. Bright orange signal blanket if you want to be found, otherwise use reflective sheet with olive green

1. Optional if tin is big enough:

a. Small head lamp (Petzl)
b. Large multi knife/tool instead of small one

1. Items *for the belt* or if you are using a belt webbing then on the webbing

a. Large blade

 i. Parang
 ii. Kukri
iii. Panga

a. Pistol (regional laws permitting)
b. Bivy bag

Mini Survival Kit Items

This can be placed in a small tin, waterproof (Samsonite small container)

Consider the following categories

1. Fire

   a. Fire steel
   b. Magnifying glass (this can be placed back-to-back with signal mirror)
   c. 5-10 matches or lighter
   d. Cotton wool is used to hold items and for tinder

1. Water

   a. Condom for carrying 1 liter
   b. Purification tabs
   c. Fire will purify water

1. Food

   a. Snare wire
   b. Arrow heads
   c. Fishhooks

1. Shelter

   a. Plastic bag (space blanket)
   b. Commando saw
   c. Small multipurpose knife/tool
   d. 2-3 meters duct tape (tape around camouflage cream or similar)

1. Camouflage

a. Camouflage cream (small 2 tone green and sand)
b. Mud and natural vegetation can be used (vegetation cut with commando saw)

1. Medical

a. Anti-septic cream (triple antibiotic cream)
b. Tweezers
c. Magnifying glass above is used for fire and to take out splinters
d. Scalpel
e. 3 plasters

1. Direction

a. Button compass
b. Your watch can be a pro-trek or something for back up direction

1. Optional if tin is big enough:

a. Small head lamp
b. Large multi tool instead of small one

Bush Pilot Survival Kit Example

Bush pilot survival kit example:

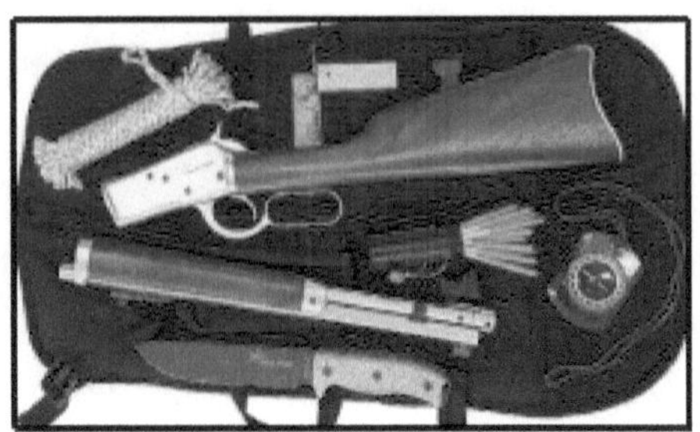

Urban Survival Bag

The focus will be moving around and entering the building to either get resources or then get away from potential assailants in your area. Your *kit for <u>urban survival</u> and <u>combat</u> survival* will have some crossover items so your kit for urban survival can be used for combat survival by adding a few items. This is by no means exhaustive, as *your situation will <u>differ</u> which means your <u>needs are different</u>*. Your situation might be more volatile, and you expect more combat, this means you might want a short pistol carbine for added firepower. How you carry will vary in your area, laws, and needs. By area I mean: will a heavy jacket stick out and be obvious or is it very cold and you can carry covert vest and a carbine under a jacket?

1. Keep the kit 15-20 kg max *depending on your fitness*. Otherwise keep it to 10kg if possible, in a medium to small bag as it's urban survival. It doesn't have to be camouflage but have a camouflage rain cover in the event you need to insert into some vegetation in a park.
2. Prybar medium size (you don't need a large one): this opens doors, boxes etc.
3. Lock pick for getting access to facilities *quietly*.
4. Strobe light (**very bright** /as bright as you can get) (non-lethal means of defense), this light can be debilitating and if bright enough can for a *few seconds incapacitate a person*.
5. **Gas canister** (CS or Pepper gas/see below): this will disperse a crowd or if you want to brake contact with a group and they don't have gas masks e.g., taking a side alley and dropping a gas canister will help you evade a crowd.
6. **Gas mask,** once you use *CS gas* canister, this can disperse a crowd and in the correct context allow you to break

contact with the crowd. Combining the smoke and a weapon could be fairly effective.

7. Cable ties

8. NV or Thermal (night travel if lights are out when civil services go out), this will give you an edge in a hostile area or if you want to travel incognito.

9. Gloves (there are lots of *rusty metal items and glass* in a civil unrest type scenario).

10. Knee pads for glass on the ground as there will be lots of that laying around.

11. *Large fighting knife* (this is *not so much for survival tasks*; you should have a *smaller survival knife* as shown elsewhere in this manual for that).

12. Light reliable robust pistol (backup pistol). If you have 2 pistols, make sure they take the same ammunition and magazines. For example, you can have two Glock 19s. Reasons for this include:

    a. you need a light back up

    b. you need a second weapon if the first breaks

    c. multiple combat situations will mean a lot of shooting (solo combat) *heat will build up in a single weapon*

    d. one in each hand means you have 30 rounds in your hands not just 15 rounds. This will not be used like a gangster but as taught in my pistol manual (see it on Amazon or contact me for a copy)

    e. weapon on left side and on right side means if attackers grab you right or left arm then you have a backup to engage the attackers

    f. this is for *maximum SHTF not just a little civil unrest*.

13. Multipurpose knife (good quality)
14. *Water purifier*/ filter,
    a. **metal canister** to boil water (this should be used, when possible, to conserve your resources)
    b. water purifying tabs
15. *Cap and sunglasses* for cover when *going covert*
16. **Combat glasses/goggles**
17. Reversable jacket with two colors for *going covert.* One side must be very light color and the other a dark color. For instance, navy blue and cream on other side
18. A wig for *going covert.* Do not make it the same color as your hair, ideally the opposite color
19. Shemagh for **going covert** (used around the head and face)
20. Dried meat/oats/honey
21. **Small monocular** (to recon ahead or from a vantage point)
22. Small medical kit, geared towards infections, stab and gunshot wounds due to presence of criminals and hooligans (civil unrest SHTF scenario). Have potassium permanganate for purification.
23. Map of the city
24. **Smoke canister** if available can be a benefit if wanting to break contact with a rowdy crowd, used similarly to the gas canister, this is just more to *obscure you from view*
25. Small notepad with pencil for intel gathering
26. Unlike combat survival you don't need a camouflage uniform, but it won't hurt to have one in your bag (overall is easiest to carry)
27. Camera (small/light/robust): record position of resources trees fruit bearing, people, places entrances to a specific venue (this will be part of your **reconnaissance and intel** gathering for the team if you have one)

Prybar:

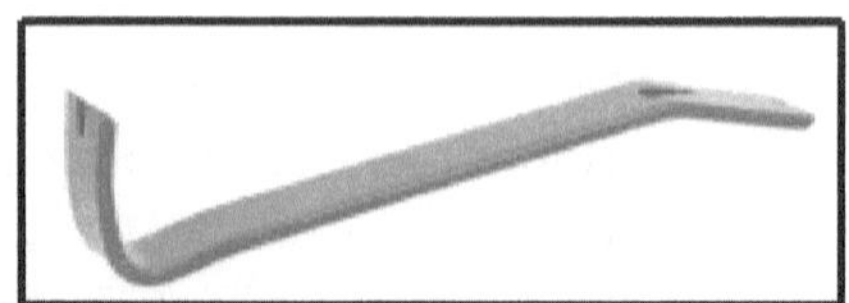

Shemagh (this makes it hard for Computer AI to pick up your facial features)

Gas mask options:

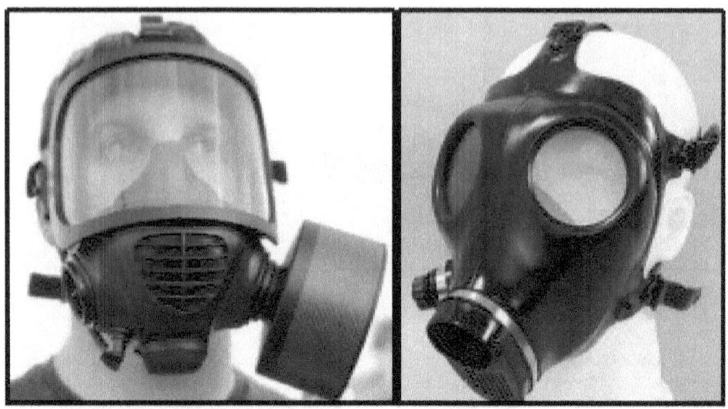

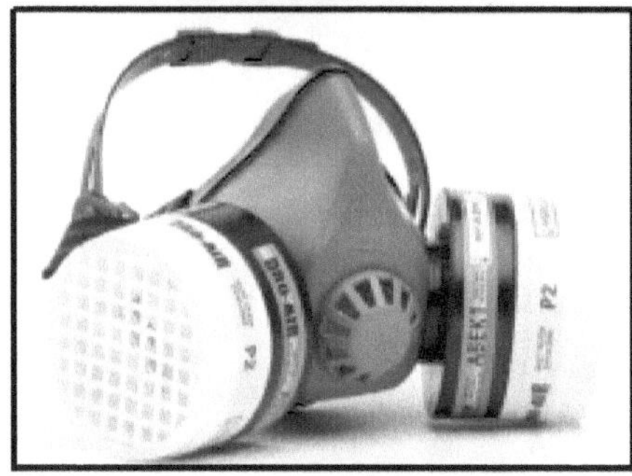

Combat glasses/goggles:

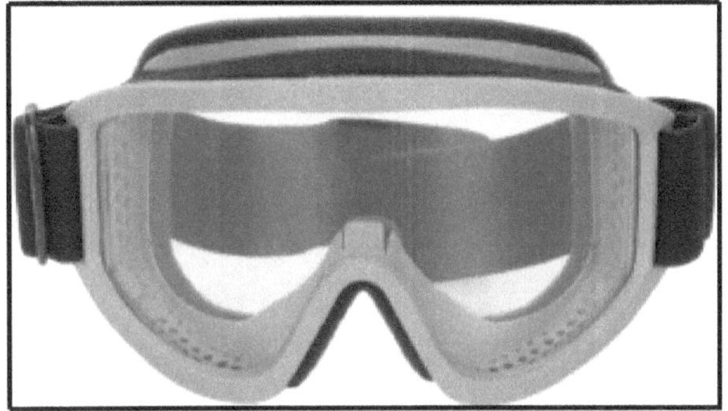

CS gas or smoke (see defense technologies and combined tactical systems):

Effects of CS gas on crowd:

Smoke grenade:

Effects of smoke on crowd, as can be seen below you cannot see anything behind the group of people:

Large combat knife or cane sword (more covert) (keep in mind *this is not a survival knife,* which is intended for small survival tasks, a cane sword is for fighting or self-defense):

Vehicle Survival Equipment

Vehicle survival kit can be more comprehensive than what you can carry in your backpack. Here you can also have a lot more food and water. The weight of the equipment can also be heavier and more numerous e.g., having two axes and 2 or 3 saws, which would be difficult in a backpack type scenario. The below picture only depicts a few items but is not fully comprehensive.

Shelter

Shelter Overview

Keep in mind your first shelter is always going to be **your clothing,** which should be well thought out as to what your environment will be. Even deserts need some warm clothing, for night times can get very cold. Jungles can be very wet and therefore it's going to be cold if you can't dry off.

Examples of types of shelter

From left to right: debris shelter, Gortex small sleep system, tarp shelter:

Light weight mesh tent shelter

<u>**Shelter**</u> should be **quick to make as shown left (debris shelter)** and maintain. Keep in mind several types of shelter are going to be applied in different contexts. *The less energy you expend building or putting up the shelter the more energy you will have* to catch food or make a fire.

Quick Shelters

These are expedient and *save precious energy* and *time* which can be used for planning, collecting firewood, or **cleaning your weapon:**

1. shelter and ground sheet (tie rope between 2 trees and suspend a ground sheet from it)
2. parachute
3. plastic bag/sheeting (large)
4. natural shelters (these are quick because they are found in nature)
5. vegetation such as palm leaves or a wooden structure covered moss
6. caves (these will be obvious)
7. fallen trees
8. holes (made by bush pigs such as warthog) but make sure it's not occupied by an animal first
9. inside a large bush

Permanent Shelters

a. Log cabin (not for tactical purposes only survival)

b. Caves (***not for tactical/combat purposes*** unless concealed, only survival). Only use in a SHTF if it's not a known cave (very small) very isolated and the situation demands you get warm and out rain

c. Abandoned house (not for tactical purposes only for survival)

d. Underground shelter

e. High shelter (trees, ledges with caves), any ***viable ledge*** with enough space to be safe as falling from a height can be very dangerous.

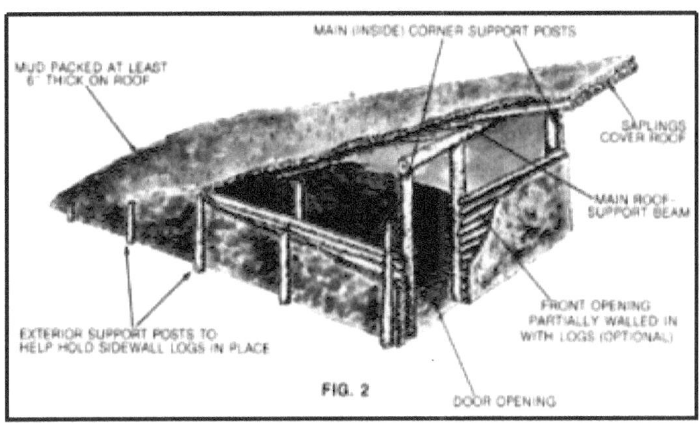

MAIN (INSIDE) CORNER SUPPORT POSTS
MUD PACKED AT LEAST 6" THICK ON ROOF
SAPLINGS COVER ROOF
MAIN ROOF-SUPPORT BEAM
EXTERIOR SUPPORT POSTS TO HELP HOLD SIDEWALL LOGS IN PLACE
FRONT OPENING PARTIALLY WALLED IN WITH LOGS (OPTIONAL)
FIG. 2
DOOR OPENING

Planning Your Shelter

Things to consider when you make a shelter:

1. ***Which direction is the wind coming from?*** This is because you don't want any campfire smoke coming into the shelter. Wind coming into the tent or shelter will also cause you to be cold, due to loss of heat through convection.

2. ***How far is the shelter from water*** both to be able to collect the water and not to be too cold? Being too close to the water normally means being deeper in the valley which also normally means it will be colder. Therefore, you might want to be about 100-200 meters from the water.

3. ***Which direction will the <u>rain</u> come from***, and can it rain into your shelter? This rain will make you wet and will also make you cold and you won't be able to sleep and this in turn will make you fatigued and fatigue damages your immune system and make you more vulnerable to colds and other diseases.

4. ***Are there any disease-causing insects in the area? Close to water might mean lots of mosquitoes***, so if it's not a combat situation then you can use part of an ant hill to burn, and this will chase the mosquitoes away so consider a fire with some sort of insect repellent which can be ant hill or dung. Some plants can also chase away insects, but you will need local knowledge which might not be available to you.

5. ***Are there any wild animals in the area*** e.g., snakes, lions, rhinos, hippos (extremely dangerous near rivers) etc. If there are wild animals in the area, then you might need to place ***thorn bushes*** around your camp to stop wild animals

from visiting. You might have a fire going to also assists in keeping wild animals at bay, if the situation is a non-combat situation.

6. For a slightly milder temperature you don't want to move too low in a valley but rather higher up where it will be warmer. Camp about 100-200 meters above the stream, if possible, as the frigid air will sink therefore the closer to the stream will be colder. This is also important in case the river should flood. ***Know <u>the characteristics</u> of the rivers in the area*** and their potential for flash flooding. This will dictate how you make your bed and where you place it.

a. Must your bed or tent be ***high*** such as a hammock or in a tree as in a tree house type camp? Your sleeping place for the night might need to be on a ledge next to a river in the event the water rises.

b. Low on the ground with mosquito net is possible but ***not in Africa*** because there are too many ***dangerous animals in the wild*** and this could be catastrophic if there are no thorn bushes around your camp to protect you at night. Make a plan to secure your camp if you can.

c. ***Exceedingly high*** (cave, tree) away from ***large predators*** (lion, leopard, hyena) and browsers that can also kill such as hippo and elephant.

d. Consider a standard or a normal survival shelter such as a lean-to shelter, which is easy to make but not necessarily best for African environment due to wild predators. A lean-to would work in America or Europe but not Africa unless you put ***thorn bushes*** in front and sides and behind this lean-to. This might even be how you make the shelter on a ledge to avoid large predators that can climb.

e. If it is a ***combat environment*** then it will be ***a low-profile*** *shelter setup*. This is to attract less attention from the enemy.

i.   Should it be a hole in the ground to protect from incoming enemy fire?
ii. Should it be very concealed as in E&E or reconnaissance or when in OP/LP?

Shelter location tips

Don't make your shelter too <u>close to</u> an <u>African river</u> in an environment and where ***crocodiles and hippos*** are you might wake up with a surprise. A shelter will be warmer a little higher up in a valley about 20 meters from the bottom where the river is, this area will be warmer because of evaporation from the water surface. Consider making it on a ledge or on a rock shelf for safety and a view of surroundings to look for wild game, animal paths to water, predators, other people, hunters, and poachers who ***can be dangerous*** etc.

Shelter location tips

Do not make your shelter too close to a river in a mild or cold environment. This is where it is colder at night so make it 100 meters away or 5-10 meters elevation above the river.

Hippos kill more people in Africa each year than lions. Crocodiles are also very dangerous. Their geographic **distribution** is shown below but keep in mind *they can escape from parks and zoos* so they can be found more widely:

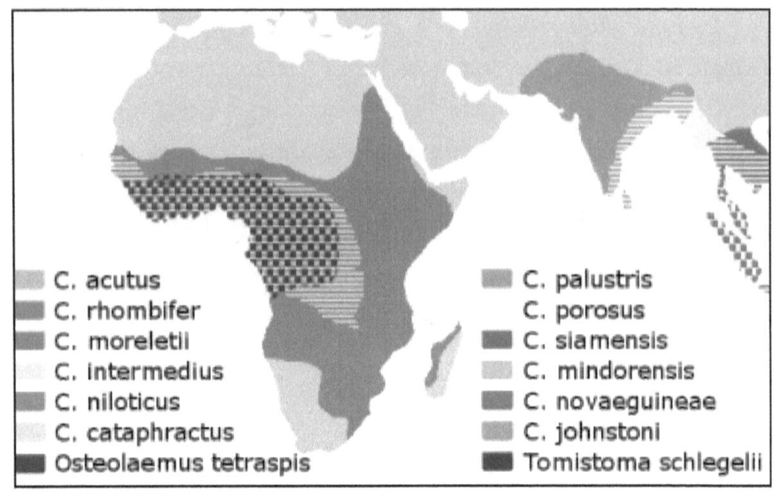

A shelter will be warmer a little higher up in a valley about 20-30 meters above a river. In very hot environments such as the African savannah this will not be so relevant. This will be more relevant in colder environments.

The desert can get very cold at night time, but you don't have many high mountains with valleys where this elevation issue will be relevant. This will apply more to more mountainous areas.

In the jungle you need to keep off the ground as it's crawling with insects, this will be a priority.

Shelter Construction Checklist

This would be for a shelter that is covered and will maintain a **good even temperature** that will be cool in heat and warm in cold. Make sure it is also **well concealed**; this applies especially to SHTF type scenarios. This does take a bit of time to do, so is only viable in situations where you are going to be in the area for a while, which could be 1 or more days. Keep in mind if you have *excellent camouflage* as well, then it increases your chances of being and staying concealed. This means **good shelter camo** and **good personal camo** is going to increase your chances of remaining covert.

1. You can use this acronym for a guide for shelters in SHTF environment (ALDLSM)
    a. **Appropriate camouflage** (light sandy for desert and *olive green* for *jungle* and mountain with vegetation).
    b. Use **local vegetation** to blend into environment better but cover any white areas where you cut off the branches.
    c. **Don't walk in open,** if possible, when moving towards your shelter.
    d. Use a **low silhouette** or profile when making the shelter.
    e. Use a **secluded area**, away from people where they might be walking or coming to a river where foot traffic will be more. This doesn't mean a bush in the middle of no man's land as this means you are isolated. It should be in and amongst other bush terrain. An isolated house in not good, an isolated tree stand is not good. You need to have an exit route, this is for emergencies or E&E.
    f. When **making fire** in your shelter either
        i. use very dry wood it makes less smoke
        ii. even better a small Dakota fire
        iii. Gas stove gives off no smell of smoke
        iv. *Tree canopy above disperses smoke.*
2. The military acronym is BLISS (use the one which is easier to remember or most appropriate for your use
    a. Blend
    b. Low silhouette

    c. Irregular shape
    d. Small
    e. Secluded

The original American boy's hogan or underground house.

Quick Shelters

Put a rope between 2 trees and suspend sheet/ parachute/ground sheet/large plastic bag etc. If no trees are around a frame made with 3 poles 2 short and one long one can make a nice small but warm shelter.

Shelter sheet

This was used as a cover overhead in the SA army and can be suspended the same as the ground sheet, there are a few several types of shapes that can used such as a small tent shape over a beam going from 2 cross branches, then one leading from these down to the ground.

Parachute shelter

The parachute is used in the same way as all the other shelter sheets, you keep it on you if you jump into an area. Even better if it's a camouflage material. Parachute material is very light and very strong. The lines connecting the person to parachute are very strong, so you have an ideal start in your survival. Take all the parachute line and some of the parachute. Make a backpack out of the chute and make a shelter sheet with the rest, it should be very easy as a parachute is very large.

Ground sheet (tarp)

Like the plastic sheet, can be either hung over a rope between 2 trees in a tent shape or suspended above your head in hot weather environments. It's better if you have a layer under the ground sheet that is reflective material that reflects heat away from or towards you based on whether it's hot or cold.

Plastic bag shelter

Plastic bag (large heavy duty): this type of quick shelter can be set up quickly with extraordinarily little effort. A rope across between 2 trees with the plastic over, make sure you can get air; branches can be used to cover one side from wind and the other opening for access and fresh air. **Never enclose yourself** as this could prove fatal.

Natural shelters

Such as caves, fallen trees, holes made by large animals such as warthog can be used (**only if not occupied**), fallen trees can have a shelter sheet placed over if it is big enough. Just put a few branches over (how much will depend on tactical situation), holes will need to be checked for any animals using them and can be a good temporary shelter.

Medium To Long Term Shelters

Long term shelters (take more effort to make mostly but not always e.g., caves are found in nature) This is when you either must shelter from coming storms or you are intending on staying there for a prolonged period of time.

Tents

Tents are an option but tend to be **bulky** and **heavy**, which makes them inefficient and energy sappers. These can be carried in a vehicle (ATV/car/4x4/Boat). They take longer to set up and are therefore time consuming and ***not applicable*** to SHTF type ***covert scenarios.***

1. Modern tent materials have brought the weight down, but they are still bulky.
2. A good compromise is a single man Gor-tex Bivy, Gor-tex is breathable and weather resistant and is warm in cool climates.
3. Then a shelter sheet (poncho/ground sheet) would be slightly less desirable that that as it will be less cover and more open to the weather.

These will need a frame or pegs in the case of older style tents, they take a little more effort but are quick to put up, they can be blown over and are not very warm in very cold weather unless heated. Tents will also need to be carried. A good option if you do not want to carry a tent is a sleeping bag with a hood and mesh covering the face almost like a small tent to only sleep in. Some manufacturers make a Gortex mini sleep system.

Ground shelters

These can also be constructed as a shelter, hide or OP. The same rules will apply to all these types of shelters *in soft sand* the difficulty will be to *support the sides*. The overhead structure can either be strong enough when dug out if the ground is hard (do not get a "cave in" of the sides or you might not get out). In softer sand or soil, you might have to dig down making an open structure then **support the sides** (beams or sandbags) and then put a roof over with beams close together and put a ground sheet on top, the beams must be about size of an arm or bigger, then add soil to keep the inside cool.

Subterranean shelters

Below ground shelters, if extensive, will take a long time to build, otherwise you can make them small, and this might take a few *hours or days to build* if extremely basic, and days if it's a complicated structure. These can be deep in the ground but can be **susceptible to rain**. They tend to be nice and *cool in hot weather*, especially if combined with a reflective shelter sheet above a roof. The downside is it takes time and energy and are more applicable to long-term operations.

Natural vegetation shelters

Sturdy but quick to construct, made from branches as thick as your wrist. Can be sturdy if they are lashed together correctly (arm thickness and smaller). *They can take hours to construct* so consider whether they are worthwhile as related to weather and *safety issues such as attacks by predators*. In Africa we *build a thorn bush shelter* as sturdy as possible with as much height and thickness.

Shelters made with branches and long leaves, or very leafy branches can be cozy and sturdy and quick to construct. A shelter made from thick branches (arm width or slightly less) can be sturdy and if large palm type leaves are correctly put on then it will shed rain. With a little effort, each day they can be added to and made more livable. These can take the form of the T-pee shape, a cross beam with branches laid across from ground to the cross beam. There are many forms and shapes to make out of branches, leaves and earth. This type of shelter is very susceptible to fire, and you **should not have a fire near it** that can cause it to go up in flames as you will end up like a Christian in Nero's empire, in flames.

Permanent Shelters

This depends on the scenario which you are in compared to a standard type of survival situation which is every all-shelter type but in a SHTF situation you would only use the shelters that do not draw attention to you.

Log cabin

Log cabins are not for tactical purposes, only survival, as they will attract too much attention in a combat environment. This **can be weighed up with the needs** (too cold) and tactical situation (no enemy forces for 50 miles). This means a calculated risk says you **might get away with it**.

Caves

Caves (**not for tactical purposes** because you are **hemmed in**, it's only for survival, you can use it for tactical situations if the cave has an alternate exit or two). Use a cave that is high up, this is to have a bird's eye view of the land so you can see the enemy coming if it's a tactical situation. *Most caves will be well known by the enemy* and most probably be on a map. If the cave has an exit at the back, then it might be useful in a tactical environment.

They don't need any building but you will still have to make sure they don't contain any dangerous animals and insects such as ticks, sand lice, bats, snakes, etc. Do not make a fire that will cause the rock above you to crack if the ceiling is close to the fire, but fire can smoke out any nasties and animals in the cave.

Occurs in nature so needs no construction but **will be searched in a combat environment** by a military force, e.g., trackers, SF, hunter group etc.

Abandoned house/building

Abandoned house (**not for tactical purposes** only for survival), this *cannot be used in an E&E situation* as it *will attract the attention of tracker* and other military forces. Having said this the situation might dictate that for survival purposes you need to take *shelter out of a snow blizzard* or out of freezing rain then the danger might not outweigh the benefit. As for the cave, only use the house if it has 1or 2 covert exits to allow escape.

Underground shelter

This might be an option in an E&E situation if it's not visible or known by security forces but there **must be 2-3 exists** to allow a quick escape. This is even more beneficial if it was **planned beforehand** as a means of lying low with all aspects of food, water and access control considered. This could be manufactured or an underground cave system. Be very wary of underground caves systems as they could have bats (with diseases) leopards (in Africa) and rockfalls as well as a labyrinth of tunnels and you could get lost in a labyrinth. Stay close to the mouth of the cave, if possible, in a non-combat scenario. Use a fire to repel insects and other creatures.

Small underground hides are not the same as subterranean shelters as these small hides are small and quick to make and are more for hiding than sleeping and cooking. These small hides can be a small square hole in the ground that's covered and used primarily for hiding or observation (OP).

High shelter

High shelter such as tree shelters can be used in an escape and evasion situation if it's not visible or known by locals or security persons. This would be pertinent if you made the tree shelter specifically for this reason. This could also be a high cave barely visible and accessible by difficult means. It should also have a way of escape to be viable for SHTF type scenario or for military application.

Cold Weather Shelters

These are small shelters that *heat up quickly* and maintain their heat. You will also try to **use reflective material** to make maximum use of the heat of the fire. **To keep heat in** but wind out you can use ***transparent* plastic**, **which allows heat waves in but** not frigid wind. Transparent plastic can be found lying around in suburban areas; we should also carry this for a few other reasons besides shelter e.g., for getting water from trees.

Attempt to **use reflective material** to make maximum use of the heat of the fire; most times you will either have a space blanket or tarp that has reflective surface especially for these situations. **To keep heat in** and the wind out you can use see through (transparent) **plastic** if you have it or you might find some lying around in suburban areas.

Cold Weather Shelter Tips

Points to keep in mind for cold weather shelters:

1. Keep the **shelter small**, this keeps the heat in and allows your body to heat up the small area better and keep it warm.
2. **Reflective material** for reflecting *body heat* back at you adds a layer **above or below. A poncho** style reflective covering around you can be helpful as this insulates from the bottom and adds a layer at the top to form a pocket of warm air above.
3. Reflective material to reflect *fire heat* placed in *front of fire reflecting heat* back at you (if you have type of material available). This can be your emergency blanket, tinfoil, even metal (you might not have metal sheet in the bush, but this will be possible in an urban environment). *Logs raised up in a screen* can also reflect some of the heat back to you as a fire screen. This can be in a 'V' shape if you are worried about the wind as this deflects the wind and gives some heat back at you.
4. *Long burning fire* such as a Swedish log fire (thick log with vertical cuts see pic) this normally burns for a long time and is ***very efficient***. It's good to boil water on and is an easy log fire. Or use an efficient fire such as the Dakota fire when you want a fire that is also well concealed and contained.
    a. *This type of fire can be made from one log about 6 inches or greater*
    b. *The fire is contained and easier to handle*
    c. Can be moved
    d. *Easy to cook or boil water on*

e. Can extinguish and light again.

5. If possible, construct a stone or branch wall to stop wind blowing on to you from the sides and to act as a reflector that reflects and contains the fire heat from the fire onto you. It is a benefit all round if you have the enemy to conceal yourself from and the time to build it. This will depend on how much time you have to stay on that spot. If you have the food and water to stay long enough. It is viable if you are going to stay for a few days. It might also be determined by the cold or lack of it. Where extreme cold might demand the maximum use of the fire and heat generated from it then this would be a good idea.

1. Grass on the ground in a hollow with grass piled 6 inches

deep for insulation from cold ground, will keep you off the ground and stop you losing *heat to the ground through conduction*. A ground sheet filled with pine needles or leaves will likewise keep you off the ground, but you will need to close it in so that the leaves are contained and cannot shift out and away from you. You can also raise your bed off the ground but that means a wooden structure or a hammock which will be time-consuming and inefficient.

2. Layers of material above you could consist of wool blanket, fur (fur from Game you shot = **long term survival**) plastic bag, leaves etc. These will trap air and keep you warm from below and above. If you make a hollow, then remember that *it could rain into it* so you should either have cover above your head or be certain that it won't rain any time soon.

i. Blankets made from *wool* and cotton *does not burn* as easily as those made from synthetic material. Synthetic material tends to go up in flames and stick to the skin, where wool or cotton *tends to smolder* not burn. **Wool is also warm when wet.**

ii. This means in an emergency you won't lose your only source of warmth and you will not get burnt severely, that is a very good point to keep in mind when carrying a blanket in a survival situation.

1. Dry your wet clothes over the fire over a rock /branch because wet clothes will make you very cold. It is better to have fewer clothes on that are dry, lots of clothes that are wet will mean a cold miserable night. Even though wet clothes might dry out due to your body heat, you might get sick due to this. Other benefits are:

    a. kills germs on clothing

    b. covers your scent

    c. when hunting it will be harder for game to smell you

    d. dries your clothes.

2. High energy food (fats, chocolate, meat, pasta, and any combination of these) and water will help keep your body at a normal body temperature. Warm drinks will also help to keep you warm at night by heating your core temperature.

3. ***Body heat from a partner*** or dog will help if you have one, otherwise heat from rocks that were heated during the day in a fire especially ***black rocks will retain their heat longer*** and therefore help during cold of the night.

Hot Weather Shelters important points

1. Make sure you have the ***tools and materials*** to construct the shelter.
2. Hot weather shelters are one of the hardest to make as it is ridiculously hard to keep the heat out, but there are a few things you can do.
3. Dig ***into the ground***, the lower ground is normally cooler by a few degrees.
4. Use ***reflective tarp*** facing away to reflect heat away.
5. Allow ***air flow*** through shelter.
6. Use a ***double layer tarp*** above to make a layer of insulating air, therefore the one layer is our reflecting layer, and the other is a normal tarp/shelter sheet or camouflage sheet/tarp.
7. ***Having and drinking enough water*** during the heat of the day in your shelter will help keep you cool. As can an "ice towel" around your neck (special material you wet and wrap around you to keep you cool).

Hot Weather Shelters more specific

1. The ground in the desert will be **cooler a few** feet or inches **down.** Some militaries use this technique to keep cool in the heat of the desert.

2. Use the **reflective blanket** above you to reflect heat away from your shelter. This will reduce the heat in your shelter by a few degrees in a survival shelter. This can make the difference between life and death as the more you sweat the more water you need.

3. **Shade** will be cooler and shade with reflective material as mentioned above even cooler. Once you have applied the combined tactics you should have a much cooler environment than just standing out in the sun. This means the difference between life and death. Know these techniques and apply them when possible if you have organized yourself properly.

4. If **water** is available, you can put water on your clothes and the latent heat is given off, this cools the surface of your skin, even sea water but be aware the *salt can irritate your skin* if left on your skin too long, this will be up to you when in the situation. This is where cotton works better as it holds water longer.

5. **Two layers of material (light weight tarp) above** your head will also be cooler than one. Even better if the **top layer is reflecting the heat away from your shelter.** This creates a cool layer between the two tarp the reflective tarp and the camo tarp for covert operations.

6. Keep your *head and neck cool with a bandana* that has *been made wet*. Cooling the neck is an easy way to keep your temperature down, this is due to latent heat leaving the surface

7. The best and ***coolest shelter will be a shelter with all the elements*** above **combined**. Lots of water to sweat out and a cool breeze blowing through, and you should be able to withstand temperatures outside of 45 degrees but only if you have some sort of ***adaptation beforehand*** for heat (using sauna for instance, running in mid-day heat and so on).

Making Fire

Fire Overview

Have multiple ways of making fire on you. Start with how to make a basic fire then work on the more complex ways to make fire. With all fire making it is ***best to prepare the fuel first***.

Always have **three or more would be sufficient making fire** on you e.g., matches, fire steel, magnifying glass. Start with how to make a basic fire then work on the more complex ways to make fire. The easiest methods that you should use first in any emergency would be ***matches or a lighter*** as time will be critical for finding other more important things like ***water*** and food or ***shelter***. Having no matches or lighter means you were either caught off guard or you lost your equipment and now must rely on primitive methods of making fire. Hopefully you at least have fire steel. Even having fire steel can be tricky to get a fire started if you do not have the right tinder (fire material such as seeds of cattail or cotton wool with Vaseline). ***With all fire making it is best to prepare the fuel first***. The fire needs fuel (dry wood) and oxygen so keep the fire ventilated by allowing spaces for the fire to get oxygen into the fire. **<u>First get all the different types of fuel ready</u>** then start with the actual making of the fire by friction, lighter or fire steel. Like with most things in life if you prepare beforehand then it makes it much easier later. Some places such as the Kalahari are easier to make fire because everything is so dry. You can still run out of firewood if you do not gather enough. If it is going to be a long cold night, then gather a lot more than you think you will need as you will inevitably fall short.

Fire steel:

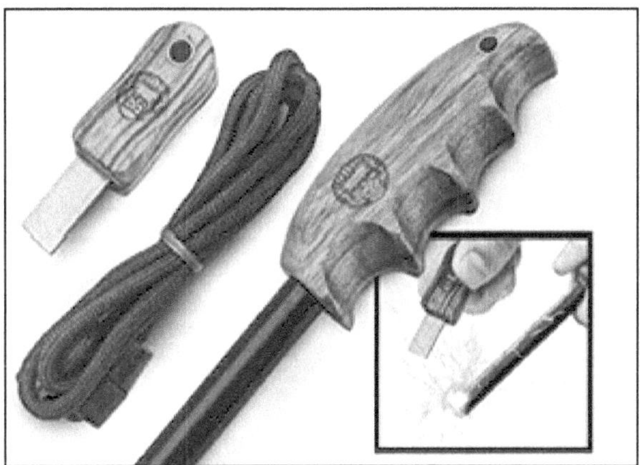

Fire Tinder

Ideally, easy to light and found in nature.

This should be very light and thin highly flammable material to start a fire; this is so the spark can ignite the material. This material can be natural like very fine or crushed grass, cattail plant (seeds head). Some plants have very fine seeds that make a reasonable fire starter. Very fine and very dry is always good, so it's an ongoing awareness that allows you to keep this stocked up. Some areas you might not find fine twigs, but if you have a piece of pine *fat wood* (filled with resin) and want to start the fire with that you can make a feather stick and use that as the fine twigs or scrape the fat wood and use the shavings.

1. Bird's nest (you can make a bird's nest out of **dry and <u>fine</u> grass** or find an actual bird's nest) e.g., very fine straw cattails/cotton wool and Vaseline (which is flammable).
2. Very thin *dry* small twigs (these can be thinned with a blade to make it easier to light)
3. Dry grass (must be dry and thin to catch alight easily)
4. Feathered stick (cut slivers that stay on the stick especially fat wood, normally pine core)
5. Dry bull rush mixed with pine resin (brown head portion when open)
6. Birch bark has a lot of oils in and is therefore very flammable and useful for making fires
7. Dried husk of coconut, this must be very dry and can be crushed a little to make more surface area available to catch the spark.

Fat wood with pine resin in them, very flammable, cutting into fine slithers is best:

Cattail pine needles that have **resin** in them and dung for firer starting, dried dung holds an ember well:

Feather stick:

Small twigs:

Using a fire steel:

For getting the fire going by adding oxygen (one of the prerequisites for a good fire), a light breeze by waving a large leaf or *light breath* can be enough. When lighting a bird's nest, you can gently wave the nest. Do not rush it, just take your time.

Tinder what it looks like in a bird's nest setup

Start the fire with fine material like cotton wool with petroleum jelly then use grass (very fine) then very small twigs (feather stick) then small branches and finally logs – for long burning fire very large logs of hard wood.

Tinder bundle example:

Efficient Tinder

Fuel types for correct and efficient fire making: **tinder such as** cotton wool and Vaseline to start followed by small twigs or grass then add small branches then logs or branches finger to arm thickness. Tinder must be very fine and very dry.

Structuring Your Fire

Consider making a reflective fire wall to reflect heat back at you, this can be useful in a few ways. It reflects the heat back to you, slows wind down a little, protects your fire from direct line of sight (security consideration). This will not help to stop a fire starting around the camp unless the wind is very light.

If you do not put stones or a shield of logs around the fire to control it, then its potential spread is more likely, you could end up with this:

Fuel Ignition Sources

Easy to light that you can buy or make:

1. Wet fire (this is good to keep and **only use** in an **emergency**)
2. Blitz (found in South Africa only, but that's the main environment for this manual)
3. Cotton wool and Vaseline
4. Hand sanitizer and cotton wool, either on its own or with Vaseline
5. Steel wool (exceptionally fine), can *use with battery*
6. Inner rubber tube of a bicycle or car
7. Char cloth catches an ember or spark
8. Alcohol swab
9. Fat wood

Fire Starting Equipment specifics

1. Fire using **matches**: this should be easy to get a fire going if the tinder and other combustible materials are prepared beforehand.
2. Fire using **lighter**: this is the same as matches.
3. Using **fire steel** is a slight bit harder if you don't use it a lot and know the subtleties of using it. Fire steel takes a little more experience and preparation as the tinder must be very easy to light and the spark must be aimed at the tinder, its best to keep the striker still and draw the fire steel across it, it sends sparks more accurately onto the dry tinder. Add a bit of steel on the tinder and then throw sparks.
4. Using **flint and steel** is difficult if you do not have experience. Fire using **natural flint** like iron pyrites and char cloth is a slightly more difficult because the flint throws a very small spark, and it is normally very low heat compared to the fire steel.
5. One of the hardest for inexperienced people is making a fire from **friction**. You need a hard wood spindle and soft board to make the fine powder that takes the heat and becomes a coal. The tinder needs to be *very combustible*. The best friction to energy expenditure comes from the fire bow drill which moves the drill faster than you can with your hands, so this allows for a quicker and more efficient fore starter.
6. Fire from **chemical reaction**: some chemicals take different times to ignite so watch it till it ignites – don't walk away, and if you do not want to wait then cover it so it doesn't ignite when you are gone. Options:
    a. Sugar and potassium permanganate
    b. Potassium chlorate and sugar (be aware it burns,

only use small amount)

    c. Rolling ash in cotton wool and then rolled it between two planks.

7. Fire using **magnifying glass** takes patience and a constant focused beam on the correct type of tinder. The sun conditions will also affect the ease with which you make the fire – in cloudy conditions you might not get enough direct sunlight.

8. Fire **using a battery** (cell phone battery, vehicle battery, video camera battery etc.) needs a spark form 2 wires touching so you need either steel wool or two wires that spark onto the tinder to ignite it.

9. Use a **vehicle lamp reflector** or torch reflector or similar device. Like the magnifying glass it focuses the light on a small area, and this is what ignites the tinder that is in the inside of the reflector.

10. Fire from a torch or **headlight <u>filament</u>** that has been exposed. This takes correct placement of the tinder and batteries to heat the filament so it ignites the tinder, you must have the rest of your fuel ready otherwise it will all be for nothing in an emergency if you did not prepare properly.

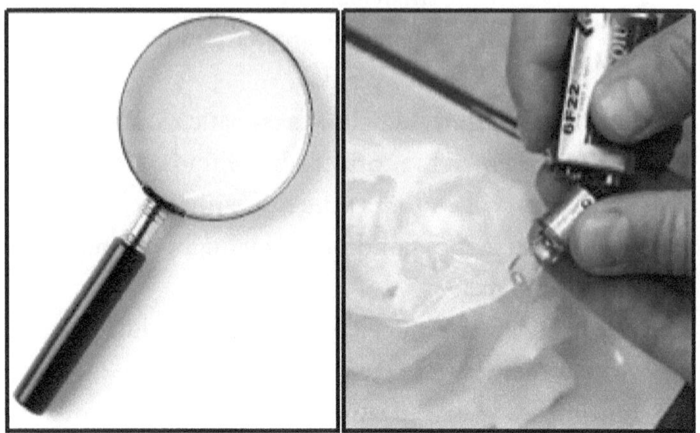

Fire Starting Equipment list

1. Fire using matches

   i. Normal matches that are not weather proofed
   ii. Weather proofed matches

1. Fire using lighter

   i.   Wind resistant lighters like the Zippo
   ii. Flame lighters like the Bic and others for lighting many fires easily
   iii. High intensity lighters like the pocket torch

1. Fire using fire-steel

   i. Fire steel on its own, this is not as easy as you need **good tinder**, you can hold the fire steel still and draw the striker over it or hold the striker still and draw the fire steel. Keep it fairly close to the material. Start by scraping some of the fire steel on the material then throw sparks.
   ii. Fire steel and magnesium, **make a pile of magnesium** the size of a thumbnail then put it on the tinder (fine wood shavings) then throw sparks (**make sure it's dry**).

1. Fire by natural means: flint like iron with high carbon content, this seems to work best with **char cloth** (made from cotton that means burnt then denied from oxygen) or a very dry and flammable tinder as the spark is not very hot or intense.

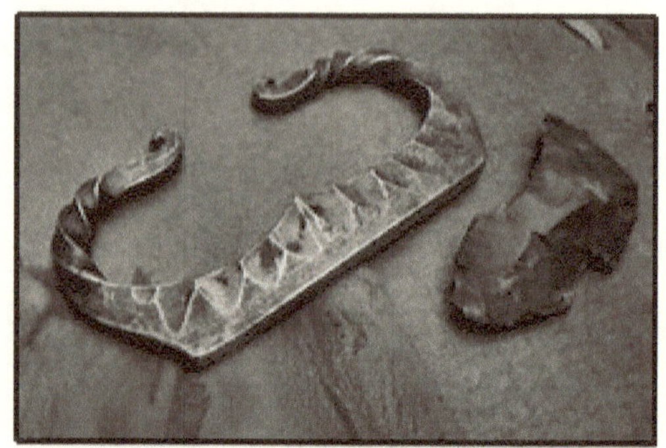

1. Fire from chemical reaction

i.   Potassium permanganate mixed with glycerin.
ii. Signal flares: this needs to shoot into or open into flammable stuff, be careful it can splash up so stand back and don't use unless in an emergency.
iii. Gun powder burns slow and hot, only use to assist to get fire going. It burns out quickly so be ready and only ignite when you are fully ready.

1. Fire using magnifying glass (***these need full sun***)

i.   Made from glass as is normal
ii. Made from lenses of a camera/ binoculars/glasses
iii. Ice (not tested yet)
iv. Made from plastic see-through bottle with water in
v.   Made from a plastic bag with water in it, this is formed into a round orb (globe /ball) and this shape is used to focus the light on the material you want to ignite.

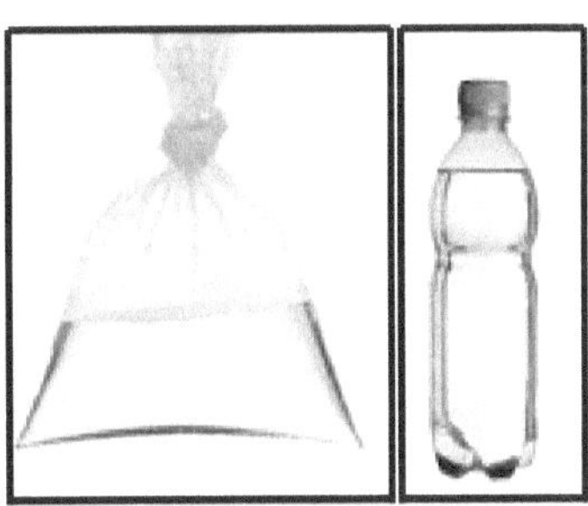

1. Fire using battery (cell phone battery, vehicle battery, video camera battery etc.)

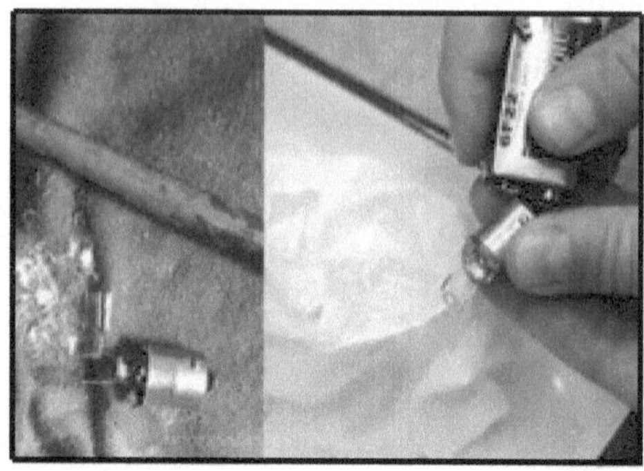

1. Fire using a vehicle lamp **reflector** or torch reflector or similar type device.
2. Fire from friction

  i. Hand drill
 ii. Fire bow
iii. Fire saw using bamboo

1. Fire from a torch or headlight **filament** that has been exposed.

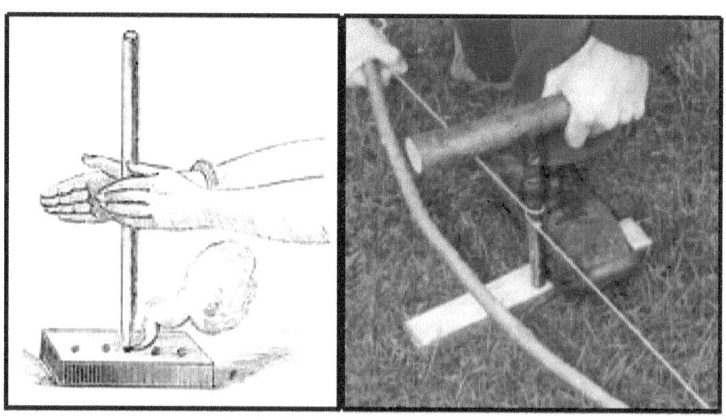

See other books on Amazon

Author Mike Harland
BASIC TO ELITE PISTOL
MANUAL
INTERCEPT TRAINING CONCEPTS

Camouflage for Survival, Combat and Hunting

by Michael Harland

Personal Security Detail Operations
Copyright © Michael Harland 1997- 2022

Don't miss out!

Visit the website below and you can sign up to receive emails whenever Mike Harland publishes a new book. There's no charge and no obligation.

https://books2read.com/r/B-A-BCLG-ZJFWC

BOOKS 2 READ

Connecting independent readers to independent writers.

Did you love *Combat Survival Manual*? Then you should read
Personal Security Detail Operations Book 1[1] by Mike Harland!

[2]

Personal security detail operations is a manual on how to conduct
successful security operation in a very hostile (non- permissive
environment). In the manual I include aspects such as weapons
training, driving techniques and patrolling and other aspects of
Personal security detail operations. This can also be used for Body
guarding operation which would not need the same level of armor
and weapons, but some of the tactics will be applicable depending on
what the level of threat is. Some sections cover escape and evasion
and tactics with regards to these

---

1. https://books2read.com/u/mgjkn6

2. https://books2read.com/u/mgjkn6

Also by Mike Harland

Combat Survival manual
Combat Survival Manual

Personal Security Detail Operations
Personal Security Detail Operations Book 1
Personal Security Detail Operations Book 2
Personal Security Detail Operations Book 3
Personal Security Detail Operations Book 4

The Fighting Rifle
The Fighting Rifle book 1
The Fighting Rifle Book 2
The Fighting Rifle Book 3

Standalone
Personal Protection And Body Guarding Manual